D0868271

THE
LIBRARY/
COMPUTER LAB/
CLASSROOM
CONNECTION

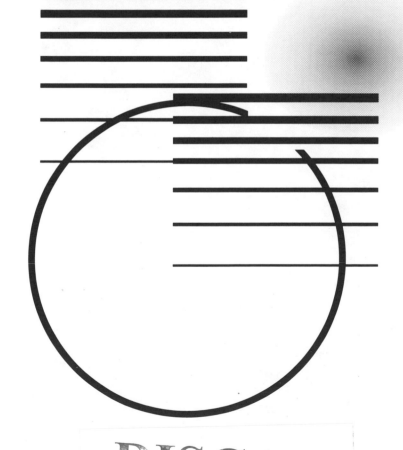

LINKING

CONTENT
THINKING
WRITING

Dr. M. Ellen Jay
and
Dr. Hilda L. Jay

DISCARD

Center for Teaching Library
The Westminster Schools
1424 West Paces Ferry Road, N.W.
Atlanta, Georgia 30327

NEAL-SCHUMAN
PUBLISHERS, INC.

New York   London

$\overset{\times}{\underset{372.6}{P}}$
Jay

Published by Neal-Schuman Publishers, Inc.
100 Varick Street
New York, NY 10013

Copyright ©1994 by Dr. M. Ellen Jay and Dr. Hilda L. Jay

All rights reserved. Reproduction of this book in whole or in
part, without written permission of the publisher is prohibited.

Printed and bound in the United States of America

Library of Congress Cataloging-in-Publication Data

Jay, M. Ellen.
  The Library/computer lab classroom connection : linking content,
thinking, writing / M. Ellen Jay and Hilda L. Jay.
    p.   cm.
  Includes bibliographical references (p.   ) and index.
  ISBN 1-55570-169-8 : $39.95
   1. English language--Composition and exercises--Study and teaching.
  (Elementary)--Computer-assisted instruction. 2. Instructional materials
  centers.   I.   Jay, Hilda L., 1921-   .   II. Title.
  LB1576.7J39 1994
  372.6'23'0285--dc20   93-40271
                                                               CIP

3uT 39.95 (net)
1/3/95

CONTENTS

INTRODUCTION

Most parents and teachers agree that computers will be a part of their children's everyday life in the future. Therefore, beginning an association with these electronic assistants as early as possible is necessary to ensure acceptance and informed application of their benefits, as well as an awareness of potential pitfalls.

Believing this, one can become disturbed over growing inequities of opportunity for children to become users of computers when they are in elementary school. Access to the single computer in a classroom is frequently available primarily to the child who has completed assigned classwork. It is often used as a reward or an extension rather than as an integral part of instruction. In situations where access is rotated throughout a classroom roster, computer time often takes the student away from whatever else is happening in the classroom. The student at the computer is most likely working in isolation or, at best, with a partner. Rarely is there instructional interaction. In contrast, the use of a computer lab enables the focus of instruction to be on use of the computer as a tool to interact with concepts related to subject area objectives. All students in the classroom receive equal opportunity to become computer literate.

The term "computer literacy" is interpreted in a number of ways. Initially computer literacy was thought of as competence in programming. More recently, however, the term has come to mean becoming competent with the use of software programs as utility packages. It is this latter concept that applies to most adult computer users, and most certainly to children in elementary schools.

It is becoming apparent that even in jobs where workers use computers or computer-controlled equipment, not many need the highest levels of programming training or education in computer use. It is also apparent that the need to be familiar and comfortable with word processing approaches is becoming close to universal. Schools can be especially thankful that there is little need to provide every student with the latest equipment, the most advanced software programs, and keep up with the newest technology on the market as long as basic concepts are understood and practiced. There is relief in recognizing that routine use of computers does not require extensive training and will probably require even less in the future. Workers are able to acquire necessary computer skills on the job in a relatively short time, especially if they have mastered keyboard use and a few software programs. Learning additional programs ceases to be intimidating, and confidence comes with knowing that a bit of concentrated use of the new program will result in success.

Wallace Hannum, an opponent of teaching computer programming as a subject in our schools, does say that, "If computers can be integrated into ongoing courses as tools to assist students with a variety of tasks such as word processing, or the management and analysis of data, that would be worthwhile. If educators could use computer-assisted instruction in imaginative and appropriate ways in their classes—to teach history or biology or any other subject—that would be worthwhile. We must concentrate on the teaching of English, mathematics, history—the arts and sciences."[1]

According to Jan Davidson, "The highest of the higher-order thinking skills is writing."[2] When creating a written passage one must continually make decisions about content, sequence of ideas, and relationships between ideas and happenings; make evaluations regarding what is important or irrelevant, the effectiveness of word choices, meeting the criteria of the assignment; and make creative uses of the information to solve problems. Decision making, evaluation, and problem solving are generally considered by many to be higher order thinking skills, and it is impossible to write without using them. The more effective the writer is in using these thinking skills, the higher the quality of the written passage.

There are people who fear that the introduction of videodisc-based science curricula which presents movement, or encyclopedias that allow the student to hear the speech as made by the orator rather than by reading it, are mixing entertainment with education thereby diluting the latter. There are some people who consider computers in the same light, lumping all of their uses as games. A neighbor who had cautiously saved her grocery store cash register receipts for a local school's computer purchasing drive expressed misgivings about the campaign. After listening to a description and seeing slides of the program in place in that school, she admitted, "I thought it was a bad idea to have computers in school. I thought it merely meant playing games. Now I can see how they work as a tool to enhance writing and reading."[3]

The challenge is to use the computer to permit the student to think and to communicate at a higher level. One expects that the small child will be introduced to a pencil and paper and taught to print letters. Later, one accepts that keyboard skills permit faster and probably a better organized production of ideas. Now that the keyboard is attached to a computer rather than a typewriter, processing eliminates the drudgery of many rewritings from the top down. This can only mean that students will more willingly edit their drafts and produce improved written material.

In order for students in classrooms K-12 to experience this type of computer application, their teachers must first be trained themselves. Teachers, generally, do not receive adequate preparation in applying the computer use as part of instruction. They may acquire some skills in using software that permit test making and record keeping, and they may be introduced to some "electronic workbooks" for drill and practice. Less likely is that they will have developed skills in creative applications of programs in their instructional areas. "Few [teachers] receive more than a very small amount of training in computers, their social effects, programming, etc. This will be especially the case at the primary and elementary levels, where most teachers already teach a wide array of subjects..."[4]

Although drill and practice programs appear to be motivational for students, they are no different in content than traditional workbooks. Whether done with paper and pencil or computer, instructional activities which merely require filling in blanks or recalling answers doesn't change the level of thinking required of the student. In both cases it is minimal. "The director of software evaluation for one of the largest school systems in the U.S. claims that only 200 of 10,000 available programs are educationally significant."[5]

Obviously, the quality of the software being used is important. It is far too easy for teachers looking for some kind of prepackaged teaching magic to grasp at almost anything that is published. People worry that the pressure for accountability causes use of programs with management components to take priority over quality teaching, and teachers will lose with disuse some of their creative skills. Even when using high quality software, the learning outcome is dependent on the teacher's ability to integrate such programs into the context of quality instructional interactions. The use of the computer does not equate with quality teaching and learning. Without thought being given to the context of their use, "the discourse of the classroom will center on technique and less on substance. This requires social, not technical, literacy for all students."[6]

The broadest application of computer use across the curriculum is word processing. Developing competence with one program allows applications in all subject areas as writing becomes an integral part of all disciplines. Adherents to the Writing Across the Curriculum Movement have cited substantial benefits of writing assignments in facilitating learning, especially in subject areas like science and math that do not normally involve such assignments. When using content specific programs with students teachers must be competent users of each program. This requires learning and teaching the protocols for each program before any productive application can be made.

There are a number of advantages when a teacher chooses to focus on word processing as the primary computer application. First, teachers need to develop confidence in their ability to use and teach with only one program. Emphasis shifts from the protocol of running the program to creative applications. Second, these applications can be made across all content areas. Third, writing requires highest order of thinking skills. As Elbow observes, "Writing leads to more detailed and complete thinking as the writer explores connections and different organizational patterns in the material to be learned and communicated."[7]

The concepts and writing prompts presented in this book have come from experience in working with staff and students in a pilot program over a two year period. Our school district wanted to determine the most effective instructional use of computers in elementary schools. Seven schools were selected to participate in this pilot study. Questions to be examined in the study included: 1) Was it more effective to have multiple computers (four) in each classroom or to establish a lab that seated an entire class; 2) Was it more effective to concentrate instruction at grades two and three or four and five; 3) Was it more effective to focus computer use on supporting writing across the curriculum or to interact with problem solving and content related programs.

Our school elected to focus on grades four and five, and to address writing across the curriculum in a lab format. We selected the upper grades because of the strength of the teachers and our intuition that the older students would benefit more because of having greater background knowledge and skills to work with. We chose the lab because, although priority in scheduling would be given to grades four and five, exposure could be provided for all grade levels. Four computers in individual classrooms could be used only by students in those classrooms. Writing across the curriculum was selected because it meshed with all-school goals and our belief that writing was the application that would benefit the students the most in preparing them for middle school.

We were provided with 28 Apple GS computers, seven ImageWriter II printers, four print sharing devices, LCD projection device, and lab sets of software for *Magic Slate, Children's Writing and Publishing, Superprint,* and *Communikeys.* Training would be provided for classroom teachers at grades four and five, the media specialist, and the reading teacher.

In accepting participation in the pilot program, we agreed to devote a minimum of two hours a week for each fourth and fifth grade class to use the lab in support of writing activities. Attitudes varied widely among the classroom teachers who would be involved with the pilot program. Teachers who had experienced computer labs in other schools were eager to regain access to a lab. In contrast, the two hours in the lab was viewed by other teachers as an add-on which cut into valuable instruction time. Teachers were provided with four days of training before the start of the new school year. Each program was demonstrated for the group, hands-on practice was provided, and instructional applications were brainstormed. Time was provided for the teachers to create classroom sets of data discs for each of the programs. Introducing the students to the lab was done collaboratively by the classroom teachers and the media specialist. As individual teachers developed increased confidence in their ability to manage the lab, they took greater responsibility for instruction. Collaborative planning continued to play a major role in designing appropriate writing prompts: activities, discussions and assignments that would lead to writing.

The result of the pilot program county-wide found no great difference in teacher preference for lab or classroom installations because, in either format, the pilot teacher's access to computers was greatly increased. Also, they experienced only one format and they liked what they had. The cost factor supported the establishment of labs, but more importantly, access with this configuration was available throughout the school rather than being limited to specific classrooms. Effective instruction could be provided at all grade levels studied, but the major outcome of evaluation was the advantage of focusing on writing over problem solving and content support. The primary reason for this was that teachers could quickly develop confidence in using the word processing programs. It was much more difficult for teachers to develop confidence in using the wide variety of programs required to support problem solving activities and content objectives.

The purpose of this book is to help teachers develop positive attitudes toward using computers for writing to reach instructional objectives across the curriculum. It also addresses instructional techniques and issues related to classroom and laboratory use of computers.

1

INTEGRATING THE USE OF COMPUTER PROGRAMS WITH OTHER LEARNING MATERIALS

Computer utility programs are tools which allow you to interact with information. There is no inherent value in the program itself. Value is derived from the use made of the program in requiring students to interact with information they have gathered. In addition to word processing there are a number of utility programs that can also have application throughout the curriculum. The bottom line is the skill the teacher demonstrates in designing beneficial learning interactions.

One organizational pattern for processing information is a timeline. This pattern is useful for arranging information in a linear sequence. The most obvious application is associated with social studies when analyzing eras of history. After gathering information about events from texts and library resources, a program such as Tom Snyder's *Timeliner* can be used to demonstrate comprehension of the information collected. In order to construct a timeline you need to understand chronological order. In addition, there must be meaningful learning of facts related to people, events, and actions during the period being studied.

Another application of timelines could be during the study of biography as a form of literature. Upon completing the reading of a biography, the events in the person's life could be visualized through the construction of a lifeline timeline.

In the area of fiction, a timeline could be used to show the sequence of events that occur throughout a novel. It is particularly appropriate in sequencing the multiple conflicts and resolutions as they occur in an adventure story.

The same is true of story poems, myths, plays, fairy tales, or any other form of narrative literature.

The life cycle of an animal studied in science could be presented through the construction of a timeline. Many scientific experiments could be laid out through the technique of a timeline. Inventions, events, discoveries, principles, rules in any discipline lend themselves to the timeline format. Because a timeline requires only a small amount of keyboarding, the program serves a wide range of students.

Developing a database by using a program such as *PFS File* or *Appleworks* enables students to discover and manipulate relationships among isolated facts. The contents of a database can reflect information related to any unit of study. The strength of manipulation of the database is in developing questions that uncover hidden relationships. The database program does the sorting, leaving the student to focus on the relationships.

Possible applications include finding commonalities in backgrounds of inventors; identifying common themes among myths from different cultures; comparing and contrasting regions of the earth; analyzing fairy tales by character trait, country of origin, or theme.

When a database is being searched the students need to understand Boolian logic—for example, the impact of the *and*, *or*, and *not* concepts. The more practice the student acquires in analyzing database information the better the student becomes in designing questions that unlock hidden relationships.

Another utility program with a broad application is *Crossword Magic* which creates crossword puzzle layouts. The student needs to determine a set of words to use as answers, and to develop clues to lead others to these words. An obvious application is specialized vocabulary related to math, science, social studies, or fine arts units. Indeed, any content area information is suitable for creating a crossword puzzle. In order to create workable clues, the student needs to understand subtle differences in meaning among similar words. The greater learning value is derived by the student designing the crossword puzzle rather than the student who merely fills it in.

An additional use is designing a crossword puzzle based on a piece of literature. The focus of the puzzle can range from simple recall of facts in the story such as the name of a character or the color of a hat, to clues calling for inferences or a character's motivations and feelings. For example, the question asks for a term identifying a character's trait such as brave, curious, intelligent, cowardly, etc. which requires the student to apply deductive reasoning to generalize a character's trait from the specific actions taken in the story. There could be clues that call for identifying character's feelings such as "How Mr. Hofstra felt seeing his cow in the city," or "How Hendrika felt watching windmills." There could be clues that require recognition of forces motivating a character's actions such as survival, greed, adventure, or fear. The nature of the clues determines the level of thinking required by the student who completes the puzzle, and that of the designer.

Spelling words can be practiced through the use of crossword puzzles. Vocabulary concepts such as synonyms, antonyms, idioms, and figurative language can be fostered through puzzle use. Foreign language vocabulary can be used as well as English words when creating puzzles.

Desktop publishing programs, beginning with *Children's Writing and Publishing* and increasing in sophistication through Macintosh applications, offer students the ability to integrate graphics with text. The use of graphics can motivate students to write. Seeing the picture on the screen helps the young writer generate ideas to write about. One format is to select two graphics to be placed facing each other at the top of the page. The two graphics become characters carrying on a dialogue. The student writes the text of the dialogue by using punctuation correct for direct quotations. Visuals can be animals, objects, people, or whatever appeals to the student. Conversation can be developed for any pair of graphics—even a truck and a car, a ball and a bat, or an alien and a rabbit.

Equally motivational is the ability to insert a graphic in the middle of text and watch the computer reconfigure the passage. This possibility can be used as a "carrot" because the student will probably produce increased amounts of text in order to be able to pop in multiple pictures for the final printout.

Simulations such as Tom Snyder's *Decision Series* requires the student to gather information from appropriate sources in order to make thoughtful decisions. Topics in the series include *Colonization, Revolutionary Wars, Immigration, Urbanization, Foreign Policy, Television, Budget Process, Campaign Trail,* and *Environment.* According to the program guide, these simulations take students through a decision-making process including the following steps: I. Analyze the situation (What do I know? What do I need to know? What am I assuming?); II. Set goals/define objectives (What is most important to me? How do I want the situation to turn out?); III. Search for and examine analogies (What are similar situations? How are they alike and different? Do they apply?); IV. Consider options (What are the possible consequences of my options? Which will move me toward my goals?); V. Take action (Am I willing to take the risk? Am I prepared to face the consequences?); VI. Face the consequences (Have I moved closer to my goals? Does this outcome demand further action?); VII. Review decisions (How did I decide what to do? What can I learn from the results?); VIII. Build transfer (How can I use this process again? How is this meaningful in my life?).[1]

Use of *The Green Book*, a novel describing a group of people looking for a new place to live after the Earth has been destroyed, provides a parallel experience to the study of the Age of Exploration in the 15th and 16th centuries. Students read the novel and see how one group of characters deals with the problems of establishing a new colony. Researching the experience of the explorers provides additional information. Applying the decision making process as students work through the simulation requires their use of background knowledge related to establishing new colonies. The results of the decisions made in the simulation experience, determines the success or failure of their colony. Generalizations can be made about what was/is needed to establish and maintain a successful colony.

Although the types of utility programs described above provide variation in computer applications, word processing remains the basis for using the computer as a writing tool. There has been considerable research carried out regarding the impact of word processing on the development of writing skills. Primary evidence is that students are willing to rewrite, edit, and polish their work when using word processing. They are less resistant to making changes because it does not entail rewriting or recopying the total passage. Both quantity and quality are affected. Increases in quantity are initially more evident; however, sentence structure and vocabulary will improve as well. The students find that the use of spell checkers and thesauruses built into computer programs encourages student risk taking. As Skapura observes: "Teaching a student word processing *does not* automatically make a student a better writer. It does, however, make the *act of writing* easier, and teachers who have incorporated word processing as part of their composition classes have been generally pleased with the effect it has had on student attitudes and their willingness to edit. The most dramatic improvement in student attitudes seems to be with the lower-ability students. In the word processing classes I have taught, I especially enjoy watching the faces of my students the first time they see a spell checker scan their writing and then "suggest" replacements. They can "feel" the power this new tool has given them."[2]

However, students must learn that spell checkers are limited in the types of spelling errors that they identify. Spell checkers compare a sequence of letters with their built-in dictionary. If no match is found, the word is highlighted for reconsideration. A sequence of letters that constitutes a correctly spelled word is not recognized as a spelling error even though it is an error in the context of the written piece. Furthermore, proper nouns and specialized vocabulary are identified as possible errors because they are not included in the computer's dictionary.

Introduction of the spell checker feature coincided with Halloween. In providing instruction for use of the spell checker, a passage entitled "Beulah the Witch Had a Bad Spell" was developed. Errors included in the passage were of both kinds—those that the spell checker would identify and those that it would not. Students were provided with practice in manipulating the program as they were gaining an understanding of its limitations. The passage was created on a computer disc and booted into each of the computers so that every student could keystroke corrections to learn the process. Use of the LCD projection device enabled group discussions of process and problems. Text, including coded errors, for "Beulah the Witch Had a Bad Spell" follows: [Beula] the witch had a bad spell. Every spell she mixed something up. She [nneded] a vacation. She [desided] to go on a *crews*. [Beula] went to *by* her ticket *butt* she didn't have enough [mony]. A big *tare* ran down her *check*. [Beula] reached into her pocket for a tissue and found her credit card. The next day she *saw* waving to her (comepanyons) from the deck of the *sip* sailing to **Casablanca**.

When using the spell checker, the words in brackets would provide a list of suggested spellings including the word needed allowing for easy correction. In contrast, the italicized words are not recognized as errors because they are sequences of letters that match correctly spelled words in its dictionary. The student has to find these errors through their own proofreading. "Comepanyons," although phonetically logical, receives no suggestions from the spell checker. "Casablanca" is highlighted during the spell check process even though it is correct, because the word is not a word that is in its dictionary and recognized as the correct spelling.

Continuing observations of students as they worked, illustrated that the use of the spell checker was least effective for students who were poor spellers. When providing a list of suggested spellings, unless the initial two or three letters were correct, the suggested words had no relation to the required word. For example, students who spelled the word cattle as "kattle" were given the words kettle and katie, and when the word laugh was spelled "laf," the spell checker gave a list of nine three-letter words all beginning with the letters la.

An additional problem for these students is that they often do not recognize the correct spelling out of the suggested list. For example, when the word listen was typed "lisen," the spell checker's suggested list of words was: liken, linen, liver, lien, listen, lisbon, lichen, linden, lisa, lisle. It would be difficult for a child with poor visual recognition of words to pick out "listen" from the middle of the list.

Before and after school interest groups can also extend students' horizons. When there is staff available and interested in doing it, computer clubs that meet outside of school time can be valuable. In one school, a math aide met with students once a week in the lab to take advantage of problem solving exercises related to math skills. In another instance, the library media teacher met with students interested in furthering their writing skills. The hour once a week after school gave them time to do more indepth pieces and write for themselves rather than for assignments. Other examples are a group of first graders being introduced to *Children's Writing and Publishing* through the after school enrichment opportunity, as well as third, fourth, and fifth graders interested in problem solving by using a variety of software programs that encourage the application of thinking skills.

2
LINKING THINKING SKILLS WITH WRITING

Instruction in writing has changed dramatically in recent years. Emphasis is shifting from the mechanics and the look of the finished piece to having something of value to say. The ideas expressed, and the language used, receive the attention. According to William Clark Machias, "Writing has a different purpose than it had before. It used to be just a task assigned by a teacher for a grade; it didn't mean anything other than an aspect of the game called school. Now it has a new dimension, a purpose in creating and publishing. Students discover what they think about something and present their ideas to others. They see what writing is really for."[1]

There is no way to compose a written passage without involving thinking. At every step in the process the writer is analyzing, evaluating and making decisions—all of which are thinking skills. The teacher must be aware of the linkage between thinking and writing, and capitalize on it.

At the prewriting stage the writer is choosing the topic, assessing background knowledge on the topic, and relating what is known to what is to be found out. Whether the writer is headed into research for an informative piece or into creative narration, decisions concerning content and organization are required.

When asked to pick a topic, students frequently draw a blank. The skill of the teacher in developing prewriting activities is pivotal. The purpose of a prewriting activity is to provide a prompt that stimulates the student's interest in responding in some way in writing. Such prompts could be sharing a story, using visuals, or asking leading questions. Group brainstorming generates a pool of ideas which can be used by individuals as bridges to their own ideas.

The element of choice affects students' attitudes toward writing. "In a study by Baer (1987), three contextual variables that affect students' attitudes toward writing were identified: the content of the writing assignments, includ-

7

ing appeal of the topic and how much involvement students have in non-composing activities."[2]

Students can be encouraged to construct a web or outline of the overall structure of the piece to be written. Thinking skills involved include analyzing the content, looking for relationships, identifying those relationships, and sequencing the flow of information or actions that will be included or take place. As Hines concludes, "Students who are taught to organize ideas in writing so that readers can describe the organizational structure are better communicators and, therefore, better writers."[3] Instructional time spent analyzing examples from trade books and literature which demonstrate the author's use of compare and contrast, cause and effect, and the structure of arguments has benefits in reading comprehension as well as writing. Thought given to the placement of the most important reason within an argument "requires students to make judgments about relative importance of ideas."[4] This type of planning proceeds into the writing of the initial draft. After the initial draft has been written, the revision process can begin.

Revision focuses on organization, sequencing events, locating gaps or redundancies. Editing comes later and focuses on final polishing of grammar, spelling, punctuation, and the mechanics. Revision is more effective when there is input from a teacher or classmates. Cooperative learning and peer conferencing have become successful practices in many classrooms.

Peer conferencing has roots in the real world. "Writing is no longer a solitary affair. Students have not only become more involved in their own writing, but also in that of their peers. They are enmeshed in the total writing process from inception to revision. Review of the literature on technology in writing reveals that a good deal of professional writing is performed by a team of writers who work together to produce a document, but who also review and critique each other's work."[5]

When students are analyzing someone else's writing, and making suggestions for improvements, they are involved once again with thinking skills. Although it may be easier to critique someone else's writing, in time the skill of critiquing one's own work develops. However, it takes guidance and practice to develop the skills needed to critique someone else's writing. Revision focuses on strengthening the organization and content of the piece, identifying omissions, illogical sequences, inclusion of irrelevant material, details, sentence structure, and word choice. There is no way around it—this kind of evaluation requires application of higher level thinking skills. Successful communication is dependent upon thoughtful activity.

The mechanics of editing are more clearcut than those of revision. In revision there are many options to choose from, some better than others, and the end result is a matter of judgement. When one comes to editing, however, there are rules of grammar, punctuation, and spelling that need to be adhered to.

It is here that the editing tools of the word processor—spell checkers, thesauruses, grammar checkers—come into play. It is here, too, that critics of the use of word processing programs in writing voice concern. As Hilary Cowan points out, "Teachers are striving to do more writing with students and computers help, but too often teachers get enamored with the professional look of a student's word processed or desktop published document and not the substance of it. The research on word processing spells it out quite nicely: It makes students more fluent, do more editing, but quality is not built into the word processor. That's where the teacher fits into the picture."[6]

The last step in the writing process is the publishing and sharing of one's writing. Knowing that it will be read and reacted to by others encourages students to work at writing. When they find that others value what they have to say, self-esteem often improves and their output increases. They can astonish themselves by the quality of their own thoughts filtered and shaped through the disciplines of writing. This is especially true when the student believes that the writing, "Has a real purpose. Real subjects that affect students' lives (for example, a report on community recycling) and real audiences other than teachers (peers in other schools or community members) help simulate the real world to students, who may feel disconnected in the classroom."[7]

Helen Hollingsworth believes that technology changes what goes on in the writing classroom. "Using computers changes the way students write. It gets closer to the kinds of work that adults produce. Students can do more with the computer. It's hard to do 'kid-work' on a computer. Kid work is fill-in-the-blank, multiple choice, writing activities that kids do not value."[8] When writing is used across the curriculum, this also gets away from fill-in-the-blank type activities. Writing can be used to demonstrate comprehension and thinking in subjects not always thought of as requiring writing—math and science, for example. Robin Fogarty points out that, "Prediction is a skill used to estimate in math, forecast in current events, anticipate in a novel, and hypothesize in the science laboratory."[9]

Students who are asked to keep a math journal explain their understanding of mathematical concepts and provide procedural directions for mathematical processes. To be able to put this information into words the student has to think the process through. If there are lapses or misconceptions in a student's thinking, the teacher can quickly spot them. One example of this type of writing is described by Beverly Pilchman, who says that with each math unit, her students write before, during, and after their learning discoveries. Before her students even work on a decimal unit, she says to them, "Write everything you know or think you might know about decimals. The way they are used, what they might mean, or where you have seen them. You can use writing, diagrams, or illustrations to indicate what you know."[10]

Another activity in math is to create story problems. Ken Winograd tells of fifth graders who do this. "Students identified peer-generated problems as more interesting and challenging than textbook problems. Textbook problems were considered easier than peers' problems because textbook problems tend to be grouped in chapters or on worksheets according to a common concept, skill, or procedure. After doing one or two problems on a textbook page, for example, it was not difficult for students to figure out the required operation for the remaining problems. Each student-generated problem had to be analyzed and understood independently of the preceding or following problem."[11]

"Children generated problems from sources that included actual experience, hobbies, imagination, social studies or science reading, and objects in the class environment. Helping others to solve the problems they had written helped them learn to write problems that included all necessary information, although problems might also include extraneous information."[12]

Another approach is the one used by Diane Miller. She provides writing assignments that read, "A friend asks you to check his problem. Would you mark the following problem correct or incorrect, and why?"[13]

The use and study of literature has long been tied in with writing, but there are different ways of making that writing valuable. Rather than retell the story plot or events, or reacting to the story stating why it was liked or disliked, writing about a story's content or subject matter as a prelude to reading the story can be beneficial. Suggest free writing for ten minutes or so on "their own families or on the times when they have had to move away from their homes, and then sharing these responses would evoke all the feelings of love, security, regret, and pain embodied by the story as well."[14] In this instance the story is Greenfield's *Grandma's Joy*, an account of having to move. Other stories contain topics with which students have had personal experience or know something about such as death, illness, divorce, love, new neighbors, or accomplishments.

Writing about one's reaction to a story or events within it, leaves lower-levels of thought and moves into interpretation and evaluation. Recognizing the relationship of key details to the resolution of the story calls for more advanced thinking. Sometimes the relationships are only implied. When students share their views with each other, small group discussions can lead to increasingly more complex views of the story that they have read and re-acted to.

Roberta Jackson commenting on learning to write observes that, "An effective writing program would develop the 'habit of writing' for the student's own purposes, [a view] supported by others who argue for a naturalistic language curriculum. They believe that literacy is acquired through developmental stages much like learning to speak, and that writing instruction, unlike speech, rarely starts prior to school. Because students are asked to begin writing at the 'formal' stage without first acquiring skill or confidence in the prerequisite forms, writing is difficult for them."[15]

It is the nature of the assignment and the teacher's criteria that determines the quality of the written product. It is the teacher's interactions with the students, especially in the prewriting and revision stages, that lets the students develop their writing skills. The computer does not teach writing. It facilitates getting the words onto the paper for the first draft. It facilitates manipulation of text in revision. It produces a visually pleasing product. However, the content is the most important component and that is dependent upon quality thinking throughout the writing process.

It is not always easy to effect change, but you should not become too easily discouraged. Even at the college level the problems between teacher and student remain much the same. Rebecca Brent and Richard Felder see writing assignments as pathways to connections, clarity,and creativity. Working with their students they strive to "activate students' prior knowledge about a subject, establish mental connections between newly learned and previously known materials, see important critical thinking skills, and develop and strengthen creativity."[16] Although they believe that "the process of writing and language are fundamentally and powerfully linked," they point out the teacher's responsibility to "clearly relate the connections."[17] They go on to point out that there may very well be less than satisfactory results the first time a changed approach is used. Their advice is to "use the approach three times. Students asked to do something unfamiliar are likely to ignore the assignment. The second time they will consider it seriously but still miss the point. The third time the teacher will see the results sought after."[18] It is no different with young students or with their classroom teachers. New skills are learned only through repeated application and practice.

3
FACILITATING TEACHER USE: ADMINISTRATOR'S ROLE

Computer use needs to be a team effort within the school if it is to be successful. It has to be important to the administrator who then relates this importance to the teachers. This importance is communicated and increased when the administrator pays attention to computer usage in teacher evaluations, in teacher conferences, observations, written memos, staff development activities, all-school goals, and in funding.

Administrative decisions related to utilization of instructional aides reflect the value placed on instruction. Often the only flexibility in scheduling staff assignments is in the use of aides. A skilled aide assigned to the computer lab can provide support needed by teachers when working with their classes. Aides can be accountable for housekeeping tasks such as making sure ribbons are changed when they need to be and paper is supplied to printers, etc. An aide can help supervise when small groups of students come from several different classrooms during an unscheduled block of time in the lab. Scheduling an aide into the computer lab provides continuity and also allows classroom teachers to concentrate on the instructional aspects of lab use.

Administrators who recognize the importance of enabling teachers and staff to attend conferences and participate in workshops that expand their skills in utilizing computers demonstrate the value they place on computer utilization. Recognition that professional growth is the first step in instructional change communicates an administrator's expectations to the staff. In order to gain a full return from this sort of investment, participating staff members need to be given opportunities to share what they learned with the rest of the staff. This calls for time set aside during staff development or faculty meetings.

Administrators are responsible for assigning space to the various programs housed in their building. Creative use of space reflects administrative priorities. Computer labs have been started in corridors, closets, and conference rooms as well as in full-sized classrooms. It is vital that the administrator have a vision and make decisions to support it.

It is equally important for the administrator to communicate the value placed on computer literacy to the students, as well as to the staff. Recognition of finished products through such methods as a hall bulletin board with constantly changing examples of student work is effective. Our school bulletin board is labeled "The Braggin' Dragon" in keeping with our dragon mascot. Other means of recognizing student accomplishments include conversations with students during daily visits to classrooms, or a visit by a student to the principal's office to share an academic success. When the administrator uses computer applications to produce communications to the school and community, it is obvious that the administrator is a role model.

Facilitating Teacher Use

Setting attainable goals and expectations for instructional integration of computer use encourages teachers to try. Goals that appear to be unobtainable will discourage use. An initial focus on word processing has advantages. Teachers have the one program to learn and become confident with. Also, writing application opportunities appear throughout the curriculum, so there is ample potential for practice.

A climate needs to be established which does not turn off teachers or make them afraid to ask for help. "Handholding" should to be provided at a level needed to make teachers not feel stupid when they have a question. Modeling instruction such as introducing a new program or procedure is an efficient way of providing the support helpful for building confidence. Using the teacher's class when modeling, frees the teacher to learn along with the students. The role of facilitator can be filled by individuals with a variety of job descriptions including computer teacher, media specialist, instructional assistant, or experienced classroom teacher.

An additional source of trouble shooters can be students within the classroom. Students who have personal experience with computers or who are trained especially for this purpose can often augment the teacher's ability to solve technical problems. The students can help with the protocol of the program leaving the teachers freer to address questions related to content and criteria of the assignment.

Current emphasis on lifelong learning makes it legitimate for teachers to be seen as learners in the eyes of their students. It is OK when students know more about computers than teachers do. Make use of their knowledge, but keep on learning yourself. Not all teachers had computers when they were growing up.

Success Breeds Success

When building confidence, start with something you know will work for the teacher and branch out—something the teacher is confident in doing. As facilitator, be willing to repeat the process as many times as needed to build the comfort and independence levels needed by the teacher. Teachers should not be allowed to abuse the partnership. The facilitator is not a "baby sitter," nor is the lab a "dumping ground." The function is to help the teacher become self-sufficient through modeling which involves collaboration.

Schedule formal, required inservice training when introducing new concepts to the entire staff. It is more efficient to expose everyone to initial training at once, and expect to follow-up with individual and small group support. This has certain negative factors. All staff members are not at the same level either in terms of skills or interests. An alternative is to provide voluntary inservice activities, but attention must be given to reaching all staff members. One-on-one demonstrations and planning sessions are methods of accomplishing this. Decide on an assignment and how you are going to work it through.

The outcome of individual or grade level planning sessions would be decisions related to criteria for assignments and how responsibilities will be shared. Suggestions of how a specific computer program could contribute to the success of the assignment can be provided. Over time the contribution of computer utilization to overall classroom goals becomes evident.

Staffing to Support School-wide Regular Use

If you invest thousands of dollars in computer equipment it is only logical to expect that the greatest possible educational benefit comes from it. Unless teachers have the necessary support they will be reluctant to use the equipment. Proper staffing is essential. The first choice is to employ a full-time professional knowledgable in curriculum and in computer use. If that is not possible, then a para-professional can be hired to provide continuity in terms of management. Their responsibilities include carrying out periodic cleanups, checking (if computer mice are used) that the rubber balls are left in them, making sure that supplies such as paper and ribbons are replaced, seeing to it that procedures are followed, and that equipment is respected.

Short of that, the flexible scheduling of the library media teacher may enable instruction to be provided in the computer lab, as well as in the library media center depending on what is appropriate. This sort of instructional interaction results from collaborative planning between the classroom and library media teachers. When the library media teacher takes on assignments in the computer lab, it is essential that additional clerical assistance be provided in the media center. When the computer lab is not a part of the library media center, a related issue may be providing supervision for the library media center as the media teacher is providing instruction in the computer lab.

Volunteers can be trained to run the lab program, but most of the questions from the students involve the assignment rather than the purely technical aspects of running the computer program. For this reason, the presence of someone involved in the curricular aspects of the school's program becomes essential. Volunteers can soon feel useless as the students become technically proficient, and it is mainly the curricular aspects of the assignment that confuse them. Unless volunteers continue to feel needed and involved, they tend to stop participating.

KEYBOARDING

Keyboarding skills become a controversial topic. There are those who believe it is useless to try to have students use a computer unless they have sufficient keyboarding skills (for example, touch typing) to function. These teachers tend to insist that students write out whatever they are doing with paper and pencil first, revise and edit their manuscript, and then go to the computer to enter and print a final product.

There are those who believe that requiring the pencil and paper draft limits creativity, slows thinking, and reduces quantity and quality of written passages because the student's enthusiasm for the assignment is lower. They see that composing at the keyboard, even with minimal skills, is motivating. "Researchers have demonstrated that writers who compose at the computer are motivated to spend more time composing . According to Solomon, as cited by Dybdahl and Shaw (1989), word processors release children's creativity. 'When they don't have to worry about the mechanics of their writing, they can be spontaneous.'"[1]

When considering when and how to teach keyboarding skills, decisions have to be made. "First, there is growing emphasis on keyboard familiarization, helping students learn about the keyboard without requiring them to become touch typers. And second, there is increasing attention to the integration of keyboarding instruction with other aspects of the language arts curriculum."[2] As with other skills, mastery is easier when skills are taught in context rather than in isolation.

No matter which approach is used, some basics should be fostered. The use of both hands from the beginning is essential. Tell students there is a "wall" in the middle of the keyboard and neither hand can cross the barrier. Keys on the right half are typed by the right hand; keys on the left half are typed by the left hand. To begin with, students will use just their index fingers, but they are using the "two-hand" concept. Gradually, they begin to use other fingers as well.

After students discover that keyboarding is important to get data entered more rapidly, practice with a keyboarding program to develop touch typing skills really pays off. Until they have experienced the need for the skill and the impact of the skill, they fail to see the reason for or have interest in practicing.

Students should be encouraged to use the appropriate fingers for the shift and space keys from the beginning. In the interest of building long term habits, it is better to insist that students use the shift key and save the use of Caps Lock key for an extended sequence of capital letters. When students use the Caps Lock key for a single capital letter they are slowed by needing to stop to put the Caps Lock key on and off, as well as striking the letter key. Referring to the use of the thumb and little finger as "teeter-tottering"[3] to operate the space bar and shift key is helpful to young students. Students have to learn to put a space between words and two spaces between sentences as well as to begin sentences with a capital letter. Building these habits from the beginning avoids the need for relearning fingering habits.

Additional keyboard practice can be provided by using laminated paper facsimile keyboards at students' desks. By asking students to "Find the P; find the S; find the J, etc." beneficial use can be made of those few minutes between activities. If facsimile keyboards are taped to the desktops, students subconsciously learn letter locations simply by its being in the field of vision. If it is stored in a folder in the desk it does not get as much wear and lasts longer, but it takes time to retrieve it for use. When introducing a new program in the classroom prior to using it in the lab, students can keystroke commands at their desks as the program is being demonstrated. Using an LCD or large screen monitor so the whole class can see, introduces the location of command keys and their functions. Additional copies of the facsimile keyboard can be used at home for such activities as practicing spelling words.

Parents can be encouraged to provide a keyboarding program for home use, and to help students improve their keyboarding skills. Parents who type surely recognize the benefit of being keyboard literate.

The use of a school-wide honor roll related to keyboarding speed can be effective. Students are tested on entering data in a timely manner using two minute tests. If tests are given in September, January and May, or if they are done every marking period and posted, students are motivated to practice and improve their scores.

The honor roll we used had various levels: 10, 15, 20, 25, and over 30 words a minute. Anybody who improved 10 words a minute in a marking period received special recognition. Another angle is to recognize classroom and grade level type-off champions. Teachers can be challenged by any student to a type-off. A prepared paragraph is provided for use as the text to be typed. The test text is changed each marking period.

4

CREATION AND MANAGEMENT OF THE LAB

Most activities that are accomplished in a computer lab can be experienced by a student working with a computer in the classroom. The advantage of the lab is that all students in the class can be working on the computer assisted activity at the same time rather than having to do it individually over an extended period of time. As students generate increasingly sophisticated documents, they need hours rather than minutes at the keyboard. To provide this experience for a classroom of even twenty-five students becomes unwieldy. The use of a lab enables closure of a writing activity within two or three class periods making class management more efficient and learning more effective. Collaboration during the writing process can occur naturally, peer conferencing can be facilitated, and problems can be solved more easily in the lab setting.

Planning

When the decision has been made to establish a computer lab it is only the first of many decisions that must be made. Initial decisions revolve around the number of computers in the lab: whether it will provide a computer for every student or if students will need to be paired or partnered; whether the computers are to be networked or not; the number of printers or of print sharing devices to be provided; the brand and model of computers purchased; level of security to be implemented. The available budget will largely determine these decisions. In addition, thought needs to be given to the purpose of the lab which dictates the selection of software and staffing decisions.

If the primary function of the lab is for word processing and writing, the only software needed is word processing, desktop publishing, and keyboarding programs. If, on the other hand, content support is to be the primary function, a variety of additional programs including drill and practice, simulations, and problem solving applications are needed. Further impact of this decision is the training that is required for teachers. When you are using word processing and applying writing across the curriculum, a minimum of training is required to develop teacher confidence. On the other hand, teachers need to have confidence in their ability to use each individual program application. Building the necessary level of confidence to use multiple programs requires more training. A teacher becomes confident only when the program is used frequently.

If the purpose includes providing release time for classroom teachers, the lab must be staffed with additional personnel. If classroom teachers are expected to work with their students additional staffing is needed primarily during the training process. While classroom teachers are developing confidence, it is important to have someone available to turn to for support when problems arise. This person need not be in the lab fulltime but must have a flexible enough schedule to respond quickly to requests for help.

Space

If you are fortunate enough to be building a new facility or renovating an existing one, space can be designed from the start. Built-in tables and hidden wiring, although attractive, are not essential for a quality program. Consideration should be given to wiring for modems and networking throughout the building. Because there will undoubtedly be expansion and growth of technology, initial planning should make provision for expanding wiring inexpensively.

More often one must work around obstacles. Minimum space for a lab that will seat a classroom group of 30, roughly a standard class room size, is required. Most schools do not have empty classrooms; therefore, creative use of space becomes a priority. When attempting to identify a suitable space, consideration might be given to multiple uses of teaching space. Resource staff can sometimes share areas when the personnel are only in the building part time. No one likes to give up space, but consideration of value to the total school program should receive priority.

After space has been identified, check availability for appropriate wiring. Drop posts, added outlets, strip outlets, are relatively inexpensive adaptations.

New furniture is pleasing, but mixed and matched warehouse surplus can serve adequately. Tables and chairs do need to be matched as nearly as possible to proper heights for keyboard use and sizes of students. Having first and sixth graders using the same lab will cause some mismatches, but thought needs to be given to ways to accommodate the student. Although it is not the most desirable situation, primary students can adapt more easily to table heights and chair sizes necessary to accommodate older students than to expect the larger sized students to squeeze into furniture designed for primary students.

Security

The equipment for the lab is costly. Added security needs to be provided for the lab and its equipment. This may be done in a variety of ways. The lab may be equipped with special locks and limited keys, or it may have electronic security devices installed. If electronic devices are used, custodians have to be involved in making sure the system is not compromised. Someone must have the responsibility to see that the system is in place and operating at the end of instructional use. At the beginning of the school day the system should not be deactivated until someone assumes responsibility. There must be a balance between who needs to have access to the security system codes and overall security. Obviously, the more people who know the codes, the less secure the system becomes. Security may create inconveniences when the lab is used by people outside the school, for workshops at night, or for summer school sessions. Nonetheless, the benefits of a tight security system far outweigh the inconveniences because of the potential impact of damage to or loss of educational materials.

Closets and storage cabinets within the lab may need to be locked to secure software and supplies. If combination locks are used, use the type that permits setting your own combinations based on meaningful numbers such as school phone number, zip code, or other commonly known series of numbers that teachers do not have to relearn. If the materials are worthy of lock-up, the combination chosen must not be shared indiscriminately. Consistent follow-through of security procedures is inconvenient at times. However, it is wiser to prevent losses than to have to replace or do without materials. Not everyone seems to see the necessity for tight accountability which makes it necessary to stress security procedures with all users of the lab. Although it is not always easy to get compliance, it is necessary to emphasize that common standards must be followed. By doing so the users protect themselves as well as the materials.

Layout

Layout is another consideration. Often computers are lined up facing perimeter walls with a double row of computers facing each other down the center. This permits the teacher to rapidly get to any student requesting help. It also lets the teacher view the screens with a minimum of movement. It is helpful when giving directions to be able to verify that all students have followed one command before another is given. This is especially helpful when students are being introduced to a new program or function. When students are able to proceed independently, the need for group directions diminishes. If an overhead projector and LCD projection device are to be used for giving directions, providing a writing prompt, or reacting to a sample passage, the students must be seated in a way to let them all view the LCD projection screen. The computer that is connected to the LCD for teacher use should be left free, if possible, but it can be used by a student after the initial instruction has been completed. However, care must be taken to avoid projecting a student's work unintentionally by turning off the overhead projector at appropriate times.

When multiple classes and many different students are using the lab, it is helpful to use a series of management techniques that discourage inappropriate behavior. One technique is to use large cutout numbers to identify the computers. Using construction paper, which can be laminated and taped to the side of the computer, is an inexpensive and long-term solution. It also allows the use of color coding to identify computers sharing a printer. This can be helpful when having the whole class print near the end of a period. Some programs accept and sequence requests to print from multiple computers more successfully than other programs. In some cases it is better to limit the print commands to one computer per printer. By color coding computers with printers, the teacher can call off numbers so that identified students print in rotation. In this way printer snafus are minimized. Color coding the computers aids the giving of group directions. For example: "Everyone sitting at a red computer do ...; at a blue computer do ...." When pairs of students have to share the use of a single computer, color coding chairs can be helpful. Directions can be given such as, "Students sitting in blue chairs will use the keyboard; those sitting in red chairs assist." After a given amount of time directions would be given reversing the roles.

The numbers need to be read easily from any point in the room. Students should be assigned to a specific computer so that every time they come in they sit at the same machine. Also, if the lab is not networked and programs need to be booted individually, program discs should be numbered to match the computers and used only in the computer with the matching number. If a program disc turns up missing, there is a lead to help recover it. If there is a problem with controls being fiddled with, or any other inappropriate behavior with hardware or software on the part of the student, it is known which individual in each class could be responsible. Students know that they can be identified, so it cuts down on nonsense.

There is no need to have a printer for every computer. Print sharing devices enable multiple computers to print from a single printer. Various configurations occur. In one lab four computers shared each printer using a print sharing device. In a network situation the number of printers can be more limited.

When students are actively involved in the writing process, they need assistance from time to time. As a signal or indication of a student's needing help, a paper cup can be used. When no help is needed the cup remains on the disc drive at the side of the computer. When the student needs help the cup is raised to the top of the monitor calling the attention of the supervising adult. Depending on the nature of the problem, the student can continue working until help arrives. An alternative to this is having cups of two colors (for example, green and red), green meaning all is well and red meaning help is needed. By changing the cup that is visible on the top of the monitor, the signal is given. This system is particularly useful where there is only one adult to provide assistance to the class.

It is important that all staff members using the lab abide by the same set of standards and procedures in terms of handling hardware and software. There is the expectation that when a class enters the lab to work, materials will be found where they belong providing easy access and no loss of time. If the preceding teacher did not collect and store materials according to procedures, time is wasted sorting and locating needed items. It makes a considerable difference when discs are left in disc drives, returned to storage containers upside down, backwards, and/or out of sequence. When everyone feels a sense of ownership for the lab and follows procedures, frustrations are reduced because problems are avoided.

Even when correct procedures are stressed, there are potential pitfalls. When an individual computer has a three and a five inch drive, there is the potential for problems. When program discs are 3 inch and the data discs are 5 inch you have the problem of a student's inserting a 3 inch disc into a 5 inch drive. For this reason, handling the program before handling data discs helps avoid mixups. This can become a problem in instances where everyone is not using the same program.

Some programs can be booted and discs removed, requiring students to handle only their own data disc to use the computer. Other programs require constant referral to the program disc and these must be retained in the drive. Depending on which type of program you are using, collect discs after booting, or collect discs at the close of the session. The person in charge (classroom teachers or other staff member) needs to take responsibility for collecting program discs and storing them properly in numerical order for the next use. A point here is that if this is done after each class, a missing program disc is identified instantly and there is a better chance of finding it.

Students need to have individualized data discs so that they can save passages from each of the programs that they use. Each disc is labeled with the student's name, classroom code, and the program it supports. Plastic storage boxes can be used to organize discs by classrooms. Students need to understand the importance of handling discs properly, of where to place fingers, and that the disc is either in the drive or its envelope. We have the students put the envelopes for their data discs between the computer and the disc drive (for example, a uniform and specific place) so that it can be found at the end of the session and not be mixed up with other papers causing a panic when the period ends.

Legalities

It is important to stress with both staff and students the need to comply with copyright laws. Good intentions or educational outcomes are not sufficient justification for willfully disregarding laws. You serve as a role model for supporting what is lawful action.

Stress with teachers that infringement leaves them open to any disgruntled person's "blowing the whistle." That person may be upset about something totally unrelated, but they know of your actions and could use your breaking of the law to get back at you for something else. Students talking excitedly at the dinner table about what has happened in their classroom may very well be talking to adults who work for the company against whom the infringement is being made. This has been known to initiate legal action which changed teachers' behavior.

Site licenses are developed to meet the needs of both the producer and the consumer of software. There are standard lab packs available, but individualized site license agreements can be developed. What is legal within the agreement can vary greatly from license to license. When working as a part of a small district with building level autonomy, one should know what legalities have been worked out. With bulk agreements involving large districts or regional cooperatives, the size of the population results in lowering the costs.

Although it is not your responsibility to police your colleagues, it is your responsibility to provide written statements about what is or is not legal. Posting notices in the areas where computers are used serves as reminders for compliance. Sample statements can be obtained from professional associations such as the American Library Association and the Association for Educational Communications Technology. Most school systems see the need for having a Board policy statement concerning copyright issues. This statement should also be posted. It is a good idea to discuss these issues at faculty meetings or in staff development sessions.

Scheduling

In planning scheduled use of the lab, the first step is to decide what the program priorities are and what the desired outcomes are. Assigning equal minutes in the lab is not necessarily the right approach. Older students can benefit from longer blocks of time, especially when working on writing assignments.

When using the lab for writing activities, longer sessions are needed than those used for drill and practice sessions. You may put a priority on specific grades. Introducing the computer in lower grades and placing priority on applications in the upper grades is one approach. Another approach is to recognize interest and actual usage ahead of equity by the clock. One recognizes that change takes place over time, and that there are early adapters and slower adapters. This probably has some impact on scheduling in beginning situations. Obviously, one works toward equity for all students by bringing along less interested teachers.

All time blocks do not have to be the same length because the purpose varies. For example, by using Fridays to focus on keyboarding, each upper grade class had a half-hour within the one day, and the only thing that was done in the lab that day was keyboarding. This meant that the one program could be booted in the morning and left there all day. This also enabled the media specialist to collect writing samples periodically and document growth for honor roll postings. Because everyone was in the lab on Fridays, data could be collected from all classes on that day.

Don't exclude special populations—learning disabled, early primary grades. Provided sufficient structure and directions, even the youngest children can begin to compose sentences at the keyboard. After students recognize the letters in the alphabet, they can use invented spelling on a keyboard as effectively as they can by using paper and pencil. More writing is generated at the keyboard because it is less of a chore than drawing letters with a pencil. Seeing a printed copy furthers their sense of accomplishment. Passages can be illustrated with computer graphics or hand drawn illustrations. Students at this age quickly grasp the concept of using the delete key as an "eraser." It takes a bit longer to master use of the shift key for capital letters and the space key to create spaces between words and sentences, but ideas can be communicated as these skills are being acquired. The desire to use these skills creates an interest in learning them

Part of the schedule can be fixed and part left open for sign-up as needed. For example, with our pilot program for 4th and 5th grades, their times were locked in. Any other time was open to whoever signed up. The open part of the schedule changed constantly depending upon the work being done in the classrooms and the way its needs related to computer usage. Make sure you include long enough blocs of time to really accomplish something. Time is consumed by moving students, booting programs, and resettling into the work at hand. Printing can be time consuming especially if there are a limited number of printers. One needs to work backwards from the end of the period when producing a printout is the outcome desired. An additional problem is developing the habit of saving frequently enough not to lose work should there be an interruption of power. Interruptions can be caused by tripping over an extension cord, not just a power company failure or thunderstorm. The authors can think of one class that had spent 40 minutes writing and an electronic blip caused them to lose everything. They needed no further reminder to save material periodically.

Creative scheduling can include use of the lab during indoor recess. Access can be rotated among classes or grade levels, or a limited number of students may come from several classes. The schedule can be extended beyond the instructional day to promote use by after school interest groups. Writing clubs, problem solving activities, literary and newspaper publishing groups, and art and graphics interest groups are all possible users.

Decisions regarding the structure and use of the lab need to be reevaluated periodically. As teacher confidence grows, and student skills develop, needs change. Priorities of one year may not be suitable another year. The focus needs to be on getting maximum educational return from the lab investment. This calls for flexibility, creativity, and cooperation.

5

FAMILIES' PARTICIPATION

As exposure to computers increased in school, the frequency of requests from parents to recommend hardware and software for family purchase increased noticeably. Basically, it was suggested that parents look at total family use and select hardware that will use software best suited to meeting the identified family needs. It was suggested to parents that there should be word processing and keyboarding programs available to their children. The sooner the child learns the keyboard by touch and acquires moderate speed, the sooner that child will be making full use of word processing. Although hunt and peck use of word processing programs enhance the child's writing abilities, familiarity with the keyboard will move the child forward exponentially. It was further suggested that students outgrow drill and practice programs and games rather rapidly, which may make them, for families, scarcely worth the investment. The more open-ended the program is the more use is likely to be made of it.

Evening meetings for parents were planned to let students demonstrate their newly developed computer skills. At one of these meetings parents signed in on a computer database supervised by a student. The class with the largest adult turnout was identified. Parents with students in more than one class could enter information in the database for each class. Classroom displays showed computer generated products such as timelines, crossword puzzles, written work, and graphics.

Training sessions were conducted for adults who wanted to volunteer as computer aides in classrooms or labs. This program was most successful in the earlier grades where students wanted help with spelling. Older students wanted information regarding the assignment and meeting teachers' expectations, information which adult volunteers were not usually equipped to provide. The volunteers soon tended to feel useless in the upper grade situation, and the effort was not successful.

Although this has not taken place in the author's schools, the literature describes various programs in which the school places computers in students' homes for stated periods of time. Usually these plans require that parents and students receive training together in order to carry out the purpose of the school's program for which the computer is provided. Unfortunately, the computer and software programs must be returned to the school, often just as the child's learning was beginning to take hold.

Families that have the means may subscribe to a modem operated network program which permits children and family members at a distance (often grandparents) to communicate via computer. The children find this a practical and purposeful reason for learning to keystroke messages easily and well. They also must read the returned responses. One program of this type is *Prodigy*.

CDROM encyclopedias may be more attractive to families than print format. The added advantage is the capabilities of sound and movement to enhance learning. One may hear the voice of historical figures or watch footage of natural occurrences or scientific demonstrations.

Networks that present holdings of public libraries, university libraries, or school systems may be utilized when computer access is made available. In some instances these networks can be accessed at home by use of a modem. An example of this type of program takes place at Quince Orchard High School in Montgomery County, Maryland. Within the school a token ring network connects various labs and teacher work stations to media center indexes. Four telephone lines have been made available for students' use at home and the usage is high. [Legalities have been dealt with and licenses for modem use acquired.] Logged automatically, statistics can be examined and recorded the next morning.

The Quince Orchard students have access at home to the library media center's online catalog, *Social Issues Resource Service (SIRS)* indexes, four *Dialog* discs from the National Library of Medicine, *Microsoft Bookshelf* almanac, thesaurus, grammar guide, zip codes, etc.; and *Grolier Encyclopedia*. The great advantage to students and to the library media center relates to diminishing the backed up lines at indexing stations. Students can come to the center ready to use materials. Memory capacity in library equipment limits what students have access to at home. Of the holdings at this school, only *Grolier* permits text content access to the students. Although these facilities offer great advantages to the student, families have to agree among themselves who gets priority use of their telephone lines.

Parents may want to consider the purchase of a laptop type computer now that their power has been increased sufficiently to satisfy the demands of a personal computer. The advantage is that the portable tool may be taken easily to the gallery, field trip site, or library to record research notes that do not require transcribing before they are ready to edit. Additionally, it takes up considerably less space in the home.

Family decisions regarding computer purchases have long term impact on the children's learning opportunities. Thought needs to be given to being as compatible as possible with the equipment and services available in the school and in the public libraries. There is always something newer, faster, and smaller coming onto the market, but careful evaluation will help parents make purchasing decisions that will provide access to information age opportunities sensibly. And, as Polin warns parents, "Don't use computers at the expense of books. Parents still need to read to the child."[1]

6
IMPACT

When our school was selected to participate in a pilot computer program as we have said, we chose to emphasize the fourth and fifth grades and to focus on writing. Four days of staff development were provided to the fourth and fifth grade teachers, the reading teacher, and the library media specialist who would be responsible for coordinating and participating in the pilot program. These training days were spent learning to manipulate the programs we would have access to and discussing applications for classroom use. We formatted data discs for each student in anticipation of an early start in September. The County also supplied twenty-eight Apple II GS computers, seven ImageWriter II printers with printshare devices, an LCD unit and overhead, all of which were installed in an available classroom.

We were provided with *Magic Slate* for a word processing program; *Children's Writing and Publishing* for desktop publishing and graphic capabilities; and *Communikeys* for the keyboarding program. *Superprint* was provided for banners and posters and used primarily by teachers for display material around the building. Used tables were scrounged, along with folding chairs, from the surplus furniture in the building.

An electronic security system was installed, and eventually a circuit breaker compatible with the wiring in our old school building was acquired. A current model would not work, and special ordering held up the opening of the lab for well over a month.

During the time the lab was inoperable, students were introduced to the programs they would learn by using our large screen monitor and classroom demonstrations. By the time students began to have access to the lab, they were already familiar with the commands and time was saved.

When each class had its first visit to the lab, it was made a special event for which a ceremony was held. A ribbon was taped across the doorway, and it was cut by a selected student. Pictures were taken to record the event.

Initial instruction focused on expectations and standards of behavior and use of materials. Procedural details (use of help cups, where to put the disc envelope, staying in one's seat, listening for directions, etc.) were explained and expectations were established. These were reinforced by posters placed around the walls. These *Superprint* posters also had directions for specific functions in the *Magic Slate* program such as moving blocs of text, using the spell checker—things not done each day and for which students would need assistance. The time spent in establishing these procedures was a worthwhile investment that saved time in the long run by making students more confident and therefore more at ease. This substantially reduced disciplinary interruptions.

Use of the LCD Was Introduced

When directions were given to students for booting up the program, each step of the process was projected on the screen so that students had a visual reinforcement of the verbal directions. Students were asked to make their monitors match the LCD screen. The teacher could quickly scan the students' monitors and know that everyone in the class was at the same place. Additional use of the LCD was made to record brainstorming responses during prewriting, and to provide sentence starters or writing prompts for the activity at hand. Another use was to project a student's passage for revision, editing, critiquing by the group. Volunteers were often eager to have their work used.

Attitudinal Change

When it was announced to the fourth and fifth grade teachers that they would have a minimum of two hours a week in the lab come September, there were mixed reactions. One classroom teacher who had excellent experience in another building where she had access to a writing lab was ecstatic. Another teacher who had had no computer experience, expressed unadulterated dread, seeing it only as another add-on taking away from her valuable teaching time.

The amount of support forthcoming was determined in part by the perceived needs of the teachers involved and indicated in part by the attitudes they displayed. As a result of the summer staff development and seeing the potential benefits, even the most resistant teachers began to turn around. When teachers were convinced that they were not alone, had the help they needed, and would not be left floundering in front of their students, their skills grew rapidly. By the end of the year the teachers did not want to be transferred to another grade level where they would lose their priorities in the lab. Rather than taking time away from teaching, these teachers discovered that the lab writing program helped them cover their content and allowed production of higher quality products in which students took great pride.

The major factors contributing to the turn around in teachers' attitudes basically were: Availability of technical assistance when teachers needed it, and the nature of the assignments developed with the library media teacher to incorporate writing across the curriculum.

The library media teacher's contributions to the pilot program were significant. The rapport that already existed between her and classroom teachers was strengthened by their recognition of the expertise the library media teacher already had in using groups of computers for instruction. Prior to the setting up of the pilot lab, the library media teacher had created a makeshift lab one day a week in the gymnasium when no physical education teacher was assigned to the building. This was done by relocating classroom computers on carts and using a series of multiple outlet extension cords. A rack of folding chairs was brought from the all-purpose room. The programs used at this time focused on keyboarding practice and the introduction of word processing skills through the use of that *I Can Write* and *Be a Writer*. The students worked in pairs with one completing the activity in the makeshift lab, and the other completing it during the week in their classroom. Occasionally, problem solving programs such as *Factory* and *Project Zoo* were used to support curriculum content. It was because of expressed interest and some experience on the part of the staff, that the school was offered its role in the pilot program. Personal interest and availability to work with all classes led to the library media teacher's being selected to coordinate the pilot computer lab.

Student attitudes were surveyed at the beginning and the end of the initial year and found to be different from the attitudes of their teachers. For example, some thought that they were not writing or using computers to solve problems when they had been doing so all along. It had become so natural that no longer was there a feeling of anything special, but that they had always done it this way. After one class had spent over an hour reacting to a science prompt and returned to their classroom, one student asked the teacher when they were going to have their science class. That all of the thinking and writing he had done had been science oriented, did not seem to him to have been science.

The attitude on the part of students toward revising written work is very different when using the computer than when using paper and pencil. The "penalty" for changing a word or adding a thought to handwritten material is to copy the entire page again. This is a strong deterrent to revising drafts to demonstrate improved writing skills. Revising with the computer removes this stumbling block. Students are willing to write more, as well as to improve the quality of what they do write. As students were heard to say, "You just move that cursor around and it fixes all your mistakes," and "computers make mistakes better."

Rather than being intimidated by the keyboard, students are motivated. They do not exhibit the fear that many adults seem to experience when using a computer for the first time. When working with these adults, the attitudinal change becomes essential before very much can be accomplished with the computer. The trainer must recognize what the stumbling blocks are and be sensitive to how their learner feels in order to be clever and effective in providing sufficient support to that learner. As with any approach to creating learning situations, some teachers will be more skillful than others in devising computer integration into their lessons.

Statistics

As part of the computer lab pilot program we kept statistics on the fourth and fifth grade students' keyboarding abilities in an effort to chart possible impact of the writing lab on keyboarding. Each student performed a two-minute keyboard test. A paragraph was prepared for the test. Because the lab was not functioning at the beginning of the year, and we wanted baseline data, initial testing was done one-on-one by using a computer in the hall outside of the classroom. Passages were saved on a classroom disc for future reference.

At year end, a two-minute test was redone using the lab. This time, with the lab set-up the testing required a half hour per class—as opposed to approximately five minutes per student the first time. In the lab situation, the library media teacher went up and down the computer rows saving the individual student's test passages onto a class disc. A year-end printout copy of each student's test passages was sent home with report cards for parent information.

The percentage of gain for each student was calculated and average growth for the grade was computed. There were two fourth and three fifth grade classes. The one fourth grade class had an average improvement of 167.3% or four words per minute to ten words per minute. The other fourth grade class had an average improvement of 171.3% and moved from three to nine words per minute. Grade level improvement was 169%. Although ten to fifteen words a minutes is not a speedy keyboarding rate, it is enough to let beginners become functional. Thereafter, their fluency in writing and their speed in keyboarding increase together with use.

In fifth grade one class had 113.7% improvement going from seven to thirteen words per minute. Another class had 161.8% improvement going from eight to eighteen words per minute. The third fifth grade class missed one third of their scheduled lab time due to assemblies and holidays. Their average improvement was only 83.3% or eight to thirteen words per minute. The average improvement for the two classes that received full time in the lab was 140%. Averaging in the third class that was shortchanged, the grade level average improvement dropped to 120%.

Statistics were also kept for the upper grade special education class. Their average improvement was 111% or from three to seven words per minute.

The second year of the pilot program similar records were kept. Students were tested in September and June, again by using a two-minute test on a paragraph at sight. The bulk of the fifth graders were the previous year's fourth graders. The first year of the lab, second and third graders had about a half an hour a week using *I Can Write* and *Be a Writer* to introduce word processing skills. The incoming fourth graders showed the results of their third grade experiences. It was observed that the scores of the incoming fourth graders compared favorably with those of the previous year's exiting fourth graders. Statistics calculated for class growth in keyboarding skills the second year of the pilot were substantial, although they were not quite as large as those gained the first year.

Another area in which keeping statistics proves useful is teacher use of a laboratory facility. In a second school the teachers had the use of a computer lab. For the most part, their use of it was directed towards drill and practice activities. A change of focus toward word processing and writing activities is being initiated. Interest has been expressed by teachers in all first and second grades, and by some fourth and sixth grade teachers. Statistics will be kept to document the effect of the change in program priority.

7
DEMONSTRATING USE OF LAB TO ENHANCE WRITING ACROSS THE CURRICULUM

The following activities are samples of what can be done to integrate writing throughout the curriculum and to apply thinking skills through writing. Teachers should remember that the same writing prompt can be used with students of different levels of maturity and accompanying writing skills. The sophistication of the response will vary, but the type of thinking involved is common at whatever level the assignment is given. Teachers are encouraged not to shortchange younger students, and to keep expectations high for all students. The use of invented spelling and placing emphasis on content and the really good ideas young students can generate go a long way toward sparking a student's interest in writing. Peer conferencing not only improves the writing being critiqued, but students learn to deal with the conflicting ideas that are expressed. Cooperative learning skills in diplomacy and consensus building also improve.

Writing Prompts

1. COLORS
Objectives
- Learn beginning word processing skills and cursor manipulation.
- Gain a sense of accomplishment by producing a finished product.

Materials
- Word processing program.

Procedures
- Ask students to type a color word of their choice.
- Hit return and type a second color word making a list of four color words.
- Direct students to move the cursor to the end of the first color word. Type a space and the name of an object that could be that color.
- The process is continued by moving the cursor and inserting an object for each color.
- Hit return twice and use one of the phrases (composed of color and object) in a complete sentence.
- Print out the sentence and draw a picture illustrating that sentence.

Modifications
- One teacher skipped writing the sentence and asked students to use a ruler to measure and divide the bottom of the page into four parts. Then they illustrated the phrase by using one of the blocks for each phrase.
- If the students are not to the level of stroking in their own sentence, captions for the illustrations could be dictated and handwritten by a volunteer.

2. WORD MERGE

Objectives
- Identify elements of categories.
- Develop vocabulary.
- Identify unusual relationships.
- Construct complete sentences.
- Utilize proofreading skills.

Materials
- Word processing program.
- Overhead projector (LCD).

Procedures
- Teacher selects three categories that at first glance do not appear to be related—pieces of furniture, monuments, famous people.
- Project the first category onto the overhead and ask students to type it in on their screen and begin listing items that fit the category. Criteria should be established for numbers acceptable, the objective being to get beyond those terms that first come to mind and thereby extend vocabularies.

- Have students hit return three times and enter the second category following the same procedures. Likewise, for the third category.
- Have students return to top of first list and scan down (scroll) as needed. Direct students to pick one entry from each of the three lists and type these three words at the end of their lists.
- Ask students to write a complete sentence which includes these three words. Sample sentence: *Teddy Roosevelt* took his favorite *chair* to Egypt so that he could be comfortable when he was looking at the *pyramids*.

Modifications
- Ask students to move three computers to the right and proofread and correct the sentence they find on that screen.
- Another option would be to have students move three computers to the right as soon as the three words have been typed at the end of the lists. In this way students write a sentence using words selected by someone else.

Sample sets of categories:

1. Animal	Places	Colors
2. Chairs	Actions	Fictional characters
3. Buildings	Size words	Famous people
4. Sports	Shapes	Foods
5. Occupations	Vehicles	Speed words
6. Shoes	Age words	Things you do with feet
7. Tools	Sounds	Things people try to fix
8. Appliances	Energy sources	Things you put other items into

3. FAVORITE THINGS RAINBOW

Objectives
- Develop vocabulary of color words for shades and tints as well as basic colors, categorize items by color and shades within a color.

Materials
- Word processing program.
- Crayons, markers, or colored pencils in a variety of shades.

Procedures
- For each color in the student's crayon or marker set, list the color and an object that is that color—for example, green grass, red jacket, maroon car, turquoise robin's egg.
- Once the list is printed out, create the "rainbow" by lightly covering over the words with the matching crayon or marker. Color lightly so that the words can still be read.

Modifications
- For beginning keyboarders, each student can enter one color line and create a class rainbow list. If appropriate, apply the "Roy G. Biv" code of a real rainbow color sequence and arrange the shades in the color list in actual rainbow order. [Red, orange, yellow, green, blue, indigo, violet.]
- Create color families by using vocabulary for shades of a color—for example, for reds use such terms as maroon, burgundy, cerise, vermilion, etc. and arrange terms sequentially according to shade.

4. BUDDY WRITING

Objectives
- Have younger students learn from older students; provide older students a chance to serve as a model.
- Build respect between grades.

Materials
- *Children's Writing and Publishing* or word processing program.

Procedure
- Pair individual students from an upper grade class with individual students from a primary class.
- Have both classes meet in the computer lab. Partners share a computer taking turns keystroking.
- Provide a prompt that both ages can relate to. Project it with the LCD and give initial directions.
- Allow time for partners to compose a piece related to the prompt. Insert graphics if appropriate.
- Print copies for each student.
- Sample prompts: Introduce yourself to your partner (name, age, interests, etc.). Write about an experience you had with a balloon; write about your pet or a pet you would like to have; write a recipe for your favorite food; write a letter to each other sharing how you feel about your experience with your buddy writer.

Modifications
- Send half of each class to the lab and have the other half work in the classroom on an art project related to writing prompt.
- Switch activities.
- Schedule writing sessions once a month, marking period, or weekly if time allows.
- Have partners work together on other types of projects as well to enhance bonding.

5. PERSONALIZED ACTION ALPHABET

Objectives
- Improve self concept by identifying things a student can do; practice alphabetic order; develop verb vocabulary.

Materials
- Word processing program.
- Dictionaries.

Procedures
- Brainstorm actions typical for the age of the students.
- Model or demonstrate that the action is expressed by a verb followed by an object—for example, catch a ball, tie shoelaces, eat ice cream, etc.
- Ask students to create an alphabet of actions that they can do. Think of one action for each letter of the alphabet. Make a list such as: A–add two numbers, B–brush my teeth, C–catch a firefly, D–draw a picture, etc.

Modifications
- Compare and contrast actions done by students.
- Make a bar graph showing different actions for a letter when there are sufficient commonalities in actions.
- Take any kind of theme that supports different units and work out an alphabet—for example, foods, clothing, buildings, locations, transportation, famous people [for example, blacks for Black History Month]

6. MULTIPLE MEANINGS

Objectives
- Locate multiple meanings in dictionary entries.
- Comprehend multiple meanings for specific words.
- Write complete sentences that incorporate multiple meanings of a word.

Materials
- Word processing program.
- Dictionaries.
- List of words.

Procedures
- Provide examples of words with multiple meanings such as cast, ring, bug, fall.
- Use the word in a variety of contexts showing multiple meanings for the word.

- Verbally create sample sentences such as "A member of the cast performing in the play has a cast on his leg which he broke while he cast his fishing rod when standing on slippery rocks."
- Have students use a list of words to create a series of sentences incorporating two or more meanings of each word.

Modifications
- Students can suggest additional words that fit the criteria of multiple meanings. As a method of generating multiple meanings for a word, have students sketch the first meaning that comes into their mind. In this way everyone is involved, and it enables the teacher to "see" students' thinking. Frequency of interpretations can be identified and compared.
- A variation would be to focus on multiple words for shades of meaning of a word to give practice in using synonyms and antonyms.

7. PROCEDURAL DIRECTIONS

Objectives
- Write procedural directions.
- Analyze a familiar action.
- Apply terminology for giving directions.

Materials
- Word processing program.

Procedures
- Demonstrate necessary details needed to give clear directions for a procedure. For example, have students write directions for making a peanut butter sandwich. They will probably overlook or omit opening the jar of peanut butter or the package of bread. Demonstrate their directions literally and the students begin to analyze actions in a more detailed fashion. [When they say, "Put the peanut butter on the bread," you set a jar on peanut butter on top of the bread].
- Ask students to list the actions that they take from the time they walk through their front door until they are seated in the middle of their bed. Have them take their list home and walk it through adding details such as counting steps taken, giving directions for turns, doorways to go through, light switches to turn on, and anything else that they do.
- Working from their list, have students write an interesting descriptive set of directions for someone to follow.

Modifications
- Share finished pieces.
- Give directions for getting from home to school, or between locations within the school building, or between various locations within the neighborhood.

8. WHAT'S IN A ROOM?

Objectives
- Understand meaning of clockwise and counter-clockwise.
- Understand the meaning of and be able to apply the concept of scale.
- Practice observation skills.
- Write a sequential description of a room.

Materials
- Word processing program.
- Materials to construct a floorplan.

Procedures
- Select a familiar room.
- Observe its contents and layout.
- Draw a floorplan of the room including doors, windows, furniture placement, and major decorative items.
- Working from the floorplan write a sequential description of what you see as your eyes move clockwise around the room beginning to the left of the entry door.

Modifications
- Work to generate synonyms for the overused words such as "next," "and then," "big," "little," "nice," and learn decorator terms to describe colors and styles of furnishings. Look at blueprints and learn to interpret symbols used. Look at cutaway illustrations of rooms and compare with flat floorplans—for example, titles, etc. Discuss the values of each type of presentation.

9. DOORS

Objectives
- Establish the concept of a door's being a separator of inside and outside
- Identify a wide variety of doors.
- Describe in words a mental picture.
- Make inferences.

Materials
- Word processing program.

Procedures
- Ask students to brainstorm a list of doors. Keystroke into computer connected to an overhead projected on a screen (LCD)—for example, car, elevator, closet, washer/dryer, store, bathroom (use location rather than type).
- Have each student select one door to use in the writing activity.
- Direct students not to identify the door in their writing, but only to describe what you would see looking through that door.
- For the first paragraph describe what is seen looking inside through the door, and for the second paragraph describe what is seen looking outside through the door.
- Save and print.
- Have students read their passage aloud and have other students identify the door being described.
- If desired, students can draw a picture of their door at the bottom of their passage. Finished pages could be bound into a class book.

Modifications
- Passages could be as short as a sentence for each primary or special education students, or lengthy paragraphs emphasizing description with upper grade students.

10. CANDY BARS

Objectives
- Categorize ingredients that would be appropriate for use in a candy bar.
- Incorporate creativity in developing product name.
- Use descriptive language.

Materials
- Word processing program. Possibly a collection of empty candy wrappers for ideas.

Procedures
- Prior to writing, have students discuss favorite candy bars.
- Discuss what constitutes descriptive language.
- Write a description of a new candy bar you wish were available. Tell what it is made of, what it looks like, and give it a name.
- Design a wrapper for your invented product.

Modifications
- Do "market research" using a survey to determine potential popularity of the "invented" candy bars.

- Design an advertisement for your product by using audio, video, or print formats.
- Research the nutritional impact of the "invented" product.

11. FAVORITE AGES

Objectives
- Identify age-related behaviors.
- Compare and contrast privileges and responsibilities for various ages.
- Provide rationale for decisions.

Materials
- Word processing program.
- Pictures of people at different age levels.

Procedures
- Discuss advantages and disadvantages of being specific ages highlighting relationships between responsibilities and privileges.
- Student will select an age and web advantages and disadvantages of being that age.
- Student will write a passage identifying an age and explaining why they would prefer being that age.

Modifications
- Share responses and look for a pattern of preference among students.
- Share responses at home and find out whether parents' preferences match the students' and what influenced their choices.

12. BURIED TREASURE

Objectives
- Apply map skills using legends, symbols, scale, directions, etc.
- Create a story in which there is a logical connection among the elements.

Materials
- Word processing program.
- Art materials for creating maps.
- Stories about buried treasure to read aloud as an example.

Procedures
- Share stories about famous buried treasures.
- Discuss elements of the known and unknown factors.
- Review map skills focusing on the need for a key to the symbols used, scale, and standard directional orientation.

- As a group, generate lists of possible locations, characters, and treasure troves.
- Have individual students write a piece telling about a buried treasure. Include what the treasure is, who buried it, and why.
- Create a map that illustrates the story.

Modifications
- Provide students with clues about finding "treasure" in the library media center.
- Have students indicate on a floorplan where various items are located.
- "Bury" treasure somewhere on the school property.
- Provide students with a map to locate the treasure [bag of hard candies or appropriate motivational objects to share with the class].

13. CURIOUS GEORGE

Objectives
- Identify similarities and differences among *Curious George* stories.
- Identify the formula used to provide a common structure.
- Recognize the role of the setting in a story.

Materials
- Word processing program.
- Collection of *Curious George* books.

Procedures
- In preparation for the writing activity, read numerous *Curious George* stories.
- Discuss similarities and differences found in the stories.
- Identify the formula used to structure the stories (common characters are George and the man with the yellow hat who go someplace where George gets into trouble and is aided by the man in the yellow hat).

Modifications
- Students may gravitate toward *Curious George* books to read those stories independently.
- Students enjoy the comfort they experience in knowing how the stories will turn out.

14. HOBAN BOOKS SPINOFF

Objectives
- Demonstrate concept of rhyming words.
- Recognize that all poetry does not have to rhyme.
- Create additional "Egg Thoughts" patterned after Frances' ditties.

Materials
- Word processing program.
- Collection of *Frances* books by Hoban. An LCD.

Procedures
- Prior to the writing activity, students will have read and discussed one or more of the *Frances* books.
- Also, read to the class excerpts from *Egg Thoughts*.
- Discuss structure of the various songs including use of rhyming words.
- Brainstorm possible topics for additional "Egg Thoughts."
- As a group, create a sample on the LCD.
- Have individual students create their own examples at the keyboard.

Modifications
- An anthology could be compiled and illustrated.
- Students who find this too difficult as individuals could work as a small group with the teacher.

15. ADDITIONAL ADVENTURES

Objectives
- Analyze series books that have a main character appearing in all of the stories.
- Identify pattern or formula used throughout the series.

Materials
- Word processing program.
- Collection of series books such as *Curious George, Clifford, Cam Jamsen, Berenstain Bears*, etc.

Procedures
- Select a series to be used by the class.
- Have students read independently, or read to the class, examples from the series.
- Discuss common elements in the stories.
- Have students create their own adventure for the character following the pattern established in the series.

Modifications
- Illustrate the adventures.
- Bind into class or individual books.
- Read the stories to other classes.

16. LITERARY ANIMAL DATABASE

Objectives
- Practice developing a database.
- Manipulate the database to find relationships.
- Identify literary animal characters.

Materials
- Database program.

Procedures
- Use the LCD, and as a class, develop the database format and layout of fields that will be used, such as character's name, kind of animal, male or female, real or make believe, title, author, copyright date, student's name, male or female.
- Have students create individual databases using the format and layout developed by the class. They can copy from the LCD.
- Demonstrate how to enter data into the database.
- Have students, using background knowledge, create individual databases.
- Working from printouts, rekeystroke on the keyboard connected to the LCD, entries to make a composite or whole class database.
- Use the whole class database to practice searching with questions such as "What animal appears the most times?," "Are there more real or make believe animals listed?," or sequence by copyright and look for trends in popularity of specific animals, etc.

Modifications
- Use a single classroom computer and compile a total class database.
- Look for popularity of stories within the classroom.
- If the database program allows, include a brief annotation or summary.

17. NON-FICTION 5 WS APPLICATION [WHO, WHAT, WHEN, WHERE, WHY]

Objectives
- Identify content in each of the Dewey categories.
- Discover a system for assigning Dewey numbers.
- Analyze a non-fiction topic in terms of the 5 Ws.

Materials
- Word processing program.
- Non-fiction collection in media center.

Procedures
- Provide students with a worksheet asking them to identify five titles or topics in each 100s category.
- Provide students with an overview of the Dewey system.
- Have each student select a non-fiction book to read and use for the project. (It is sometimes desirable to have the teacher pre-select books sufficient in number to permit student choice. "Selected choice" works well to get students into topics they are less familiar with and out of sports, animals and other over-done topics. This also helps ensure that they will be able to complete the assignment.)
- As students read their book, ask them to take notes about the who, what, when, where, and why of their topic. Encourage them to use additional reference sources to augment material in their book.
- Ask students to write a paragraph for each of the 5 Ws related to their topic.
- Use the Dewey Classification book to talk each student through the meaning of each digit in the call number. Have them include this information as a final paragraph.

Modifications
- Include a visual representation of their topic and an oral presentation sharing their information with the class.
- Using a standard 18x24 inch sheet of construction paper have students create a poster. Give directions to lay out the following sections: Holding the paper horizontally, draw a line 5 inches from the top and another 5 inches from the bottom. Divide these two sections in half vertically thereby making 4 five inch by 12 inch rectangles. Draw two more vertical lines 6 inches in from the edges dividing the center of the poster into an 8 by 6 inch rectangle, 8 by 12 inch center section, and another 8 by 6 inch section. Going clockwise from the top left, label each section *Who, What, When, Where, Why,* and *Call Number.* The center is labeled *Topic.* A visual representation goes in the center section and the paragraphs can be placed around the perimeter.

18. HISTORICAL FICTION
Objectives
- Analyze a historical novel in terms of elements of history and of fiction.
- Identify historical people, places, and events.
- Appreciate the importance of the background research done by the author.

Materials
- Word processing program.
- Collection of appropriate historical fiction.
- Appropriate reference materials.

George W. Woodruff Library
The Westminster Schools

Procedures
- Initially, discuss concepts of historical fiction explaining the combination of historical fact and author's imagination.
- Have students select a book from among the historical fiction titles available to them.
- Have students compile, from their selected book, a list of people, places, and events used that they believe are historically accurate.
- Verify accuracy of list by using appropriate reference materials.
- Have students write a passage stating whether the book is more history or more fiction, and justify the decision by providing examples from the book.

Modifications
- Historical fiction titles can be preselected by the teacher for student choice to meet the criteria of the assignment—for example, a historical period, geographic location, or event.
- The activity could be done with a core book approach in which every student reads the same book.
- Students have to locate their own historical fiction books to meet the criteria of the assignment.

19. SPACE ALIEN BIOGRAPHY

Objectives
- Identify attributes of biography as a genre. Apply background knowledge related to science fiction and the universe.
- Match description of setting to actions of character(s).
- Use descriptive language to enable the reader to visualize the setting and characters.

Materials
- Word processing program.
- Drawing books that give ideas for space characters. Computer graphic programs that could provide visuals.
- Appropriate art supplies to create a portrait of the space alien created.

Procedures
- Discuss attributes of biographies. List types of information frequently included.
- Generate a list of descriptive words which could be used in description of the setting, actions, and the characters.
- Create an illustration of your space alien.
- Write a biography of your alien. Make sure you provide a name, age, family, description of where he or she lives, and what he or she does.

Modifications
- Bind biographies and accompanying illustrations into a class book.
- Create a bulletin board display by using texts and visuals.

20. STORY POEMS

Objectives
- Identify characteristics of story poems.
- Identify various poetic techniques such as rhyme and meter, metaphor, and simile.

Materials
- Word processing program.
- Sample story poems based on historical events.

Procedures
- Share such historical story poems as "Midnight Ride of Paul Revere," "Barbara Fritchie," "Casey at the Bat," and "Hiawatha."
- Discuss how the poetic form provides information when you are telling the story.
- Have students pick a historical event and write their own story poem incorporating the facts of that event.
- Share student's work with the class, and have the class critique how successful the student author was in blending poetry and history.

Modifications
- Have students write song lyrics or a rap.
- Look into the role of storytellers and troubadours in sharing history before the printing press came into use.

21. FOUR INTENTS OF WRITING

Objectives
- Recognize relationship between the purpose for writing and the content of the finished piece.
- Define the four intents of writing: narrative, informative, persuasive, and affective.

Materials
- Word processing program.

Procedures
- Review the four intents of writing and the structures of each.
- Share a sample passage and have students identify the author's purpose. Identify clues.

- As part of a unit on the Westward Movement, provide topics such as the following for writing: Conestoga wagon, sod house, nugget of gold mined in California, lead buffalo in herd, a flag flying over the Alamo, and an old tree in a forest being cleared.
- Have students select a topic and write four short pieces about it demonstrating each of the four intents of writing.
- Invite students to share their writing and have classmates identify the author's purpose for writing it.

Modifications

- The project can be done in cooperative groups or by individuals.
- Use a single topic and have each group of students write illustrating one intent or purpose of writing. Compare the results.
- A set of slides from a field trip could be used to generate four narrations reflecting the intents of writing.

22. MATHEMATICAL STORY PROBLEM

Objectives

- Identify story components that can be used to create suitable math problems.
- Incorporate appropriate math functions.
- Develop writing style that includes both necessary information and distractors to make the problems interesting.

Materials

- Word processing program.
- Core books used in literature based reading collection, or picture books that can be read quickly.

Procedures

- Read a novel and look for facts to work into a problem such as number of characters, distances traveled, objects described, time frames, ages, and quantities, etc.
- Write a number sentence for the problem: $10+2=12$ or $3\times9-7=20$.
- Develop a paragraph providing background information that permits you to create the number sentence and solve the problem.
- Share problems and solutions showing your calculations.

Modifications

- A book that is read orally to the class, or titles that are well known to all students, could be used as a source.
- If using unfamiliar picture books, skimming skills could be practiced to locate information needed to solve the problem.

23. MATH STORY PROBLEMS— ANIMAL LEGS

Objectives

- Identify number of legs for different types of animals: Birds, reptiles, insects, mammals, spiders, beetles, etc.
- Develop writing style that includes both necessary information and distractors to make the problem interesting.

Materials

- Word processing program.
- Collection of illustrated nonfiction animal books.

Procedures

- Categorize animals by the number of legs they have.
- Generate number sentences involving calculations related to number of legs various animals have—for example, 4+2=6 (cow + bird), or 5×4=20 (number of legs on 5 cats).
- Create the text of a story problem to generate a number sentence. For example, the story could be about ladybugs and spiders in the garden. You have counted 92 legs. How many of each animal are there? [10 ladybugs with 6 legs each and 4 spiders with 8 legs each.]
- Or you are watching kittens nursing their mother. You count 20 legs. How many kittens are there? [Four because you do not count the mother cat who has 4 of the 20 legs.]
- Or you see a family of six geese swimming on the river. How many legs are paddling beneath the water's surface? [12]
- Share the problems.

Modifications

- Setting criteria for the types of math calculations to be used controls the difficulty of the finished problem.
- The project can be used as a follow-up to units on pets, farms, or zoos.
- Setting criteria for the types of animals to be used influences the level of scientific knowledge needed.

24. WORLD TIME ZONE STORY PROBLEMS

Objectives

- Recognize that the world is divided into time zones.
- Identify impact of traveling through multiple time zones. Note that impact occurs when traveling east and west, but not north and south.

- Develop writing style that includes both necessary information and distractors to make the problems interesting.

Materials
- Word processing program.
- Chart from an encyclopedia or atlas that shows worldwide time zones.

Procedures
- Provide sample problems for students to work prior to creating additional problems themselves.
- As a culmination to the study of time zones, have the students create math story problems requiring interpretation of time zones to calculate the answers. Example: If you leave San Francisco at 8 p.m. on Monday, March 23, and your flight is a ten hour flight, what is the date and time of your arrival in Tokyo? [March 24, at 11 p.m.]
- If your business trip takes you from Boston to Rome, and then to Oslo and Paris before returning to Boston by way of New York, how many times will you have to reset your watch to be on local time in each city?

Modifications
- Ask questions about the number of hours between locations, as well as the number of times that adjustments would need to be made.
- Crossing the International Date Line, accounting for daylight savings times and community idiosyncrasies and boundaries of time zones could be included.

25. EXPLORATION BASED WORD/MATH PROBLEMS

Objectives
- Identify math applications related to the process of exploration.
- Generate word problems using exploration context.

Materials
- Word processing program.
- Appropriate resources for units of measure such as statute miles, nautical miles, wind force, and exchange rates, etc.

Procedures
- Provide sample math word problems that are set in an exploration context. For example:
- If one sailor is paid 5 pieces of eight a week and you have a crew of 20, how much will it cost to pay your crew at the end of a 3 month voyage?

- If your ship is blown off course by a gale with winds of 50 miles per hour that lasts for three days, how far off course will you be at the end of the storm?
- Your ship has a cargo of 750 pounds of gold and a crew of 20. The captain keeps 50% for himself. How much will each sailor receive if gold is worth $512 a pound?
- Ask students to create word problems incorporating information related to their study of the Age of Exploration.

26. SHOES

Objectives
- Identify attributes of shoes.
- Match shoes with appropriate activities, seasons, and geographic areas.

Materials
- Word processing program.
- Pictures of shoes from advertisements.
- Appropriate art materials for drawing or mounting shoe pictures.

Procedures
- Brainstorm terms for different types of shoes.
- Discuss appropriate activities for various types of shoes.
- Find pictures of a shoe in advertisements or newspapers and choose one. Cut it out. (Draw a sketch of a shoe if pictures are unavailable).
- Write a piece telling who would wear the shoes and what they would be doing when wearing them.

Modifications
- Bind into a book for a clothing unit.
- Set up a museum of shoes in the classroom by having students bring in samples of different types.
- Label them.

27. PACK A SUITCASE

Objectives
- Write clues that enable others to make inferences.
- Comprehend relationship between clothing and requirements of activities.
- Recognize the connections between geographic location and appropriate clothing.
- Demonstrate concept of total wardrobe to be packed (include underwear, pjs, etc.).

Materials
- Word processing program.

Procedures
- Have a discussion about vacations—where people go and the kinds of things they do. Steer the discussion towards the need to pack a suitcase when taking a trip and the necessity of packing the appropriate items.
- Direct students to choose a destination and time of year to make their trip.
- Students are directed to write a passage itemizing what they would put into their suitcase, and to use sufficient details and descriptors that someone else can use these clues to make inferences about your destination. Examples, down parka or windbreaker, rather than a jacket; flannel or T shirt, rather than shirts; hiking boots or sandals, rather than shoes.
- Answers would be the beach, a ski trip, a fishing expedition, a theater package in the city, a wedding, but not a specific city or geographic location.

Modifications
- Passages could be bound into a book of "riddles" to be shared by class members.
- Pictures could be drawn to illustrate the destination and activities.
- Select several passages describing items for use at different destinations. Use a picture of a vacation site and ask students which passage best matches the visual.
- Students use peer conference approach to identify necessary items that were left off their lists.

28. BUILDINGS

Objectives
- Identify a wide variety of buildings and their uses.
- Identify correlations between form and function.
- Write clues that enable others to make inferences.

Materials
- Word processing program.

Procedures
- Brainstorm a list of different types of buildings.
- Discuss the functions of various buildings.
- Teacher models the writing assignment verbally by choosing a building and describing what goes on in it, as well as what you see inside the building.

- When students have appeared to grasp the concept, ask them to select a building and describe what is done and seen there. Remind them not to name the building, but only to provide clues for identifying their building choice.
- Buildings that might be included are: Bank, firehouse, school, hospital, church, shopping mall, store, restaurant, apartment, gas station, library, carwash, etc.

Modifications
- Use in connection with the study of the community.
- Identify goods and services found in your community.
- Tie in with career choice exploration.
- Adapt to incorporate types of housing around the world, for example, igloo, tipi, mobile home, thatch cottage, lighthouse, stilt house, pueblo, homeless shelter, tent, casbah, hotel, etc. In this case the focus would be on the description of the construction of the structure rather than its use.

29. CITY WORDS DICTIONARY

Objectives
- Develop vocabulary related to unit on urban studies.
- Apply concepts of dictionary arrangement.
- Write descriptive definitions.

Materials
- *Children's Writing & Publishing* or another desktop publishing program.

Procedures
- Discuss what students know about dictionaries, focusing on the sequence and format of entries.
- Generate a list of urban words in which every letter of the alphabet is represented—for example: Apartments, bridges, cement, daily rush hour, express trains, fire trucks, glass, helmets, invisible (which people sometimes seem to be), jail, kiosk, late (for work), movies, newspapers, offices, planes, quickly (is the speed the cars go), rap concerts, streets, taxis, urban, view (that can be seen from a tall building), work (where people go every morning), xylophone (which gets played in concert halls), yogurt, and the zoo.
- Match words with students giving consideration to background knowledge and suitability of term.
- Have students research and write a descriptive definition of word (sentence to paragraph).

- To provide a common format for each page, directions were given for creating a heading by using *Children's Writing & Publishing*. The graphic of the skyline was placed at the left of the heading. Text in the heading read "Urban Words" and the student's specific word. In smaller type, at the bottom of the heading, was the student's name.
- The body of the page included their descriptive definition and a free-hand drawing representing the word.
- The pages were sequenced alphabetically by the term and bound into a class book.

Modifications
- This project worked well and was replicated during the study of suburban and rural communities.
- The project could also be used for extending vocabulary related to any unit of study: Foods, clothing, transportation, nutrition, animals, plants, seasons, etc.

30. THINGS YOU CAN DO TO A TURKEY

Objectives
- Use verbs; broaden vocabulary; categorize actions; celebrate Thanksgiving Day.

Materials
- Word processing program.
- Transparency of a roasted turkey on a platter (*Printshop* graphic).

Procedures
- Discuss concept of a verb's being an action word.
- Have students give examples verbally.
- Project transparency of a roasted turkey. Ask the question, "What can you do to a turkey?" and accept a few verbal examples such as eat, stuff, slice, etc.
- Direct students to begin keystroking their own list of verbs.
- As you walk around the lab, ask students leading questions to broaden their thinking to include things that you can do to a living turkey, not just cooking and eating.
- Ask each student to share three terms included in their list but not mentioned by others. Have students continue building their lists.
- Save and print lists.
- As an extension, ask students to categorize their lists and identify labels for the groupings, for example, terms related to cooking, eating, raising, etc.
- Terms can also be sequenced chronologically, hatching to eating.

Modifications
- The activities can be done individually, in pairs, or in cooperative learning groups.
- The list of words could serve as a prewriting activity for a passage on turkeys.
- This process can be repeated using words such as house, baby, present, package, car, etc., in place of turkey.

31. DESCRIPTION OF A TRIP

Objectives
- Demonstrate ability to match mode of transportation with the requirements of travel.
- Sequence ideas and events logically.

Materials
- Word processing program.
- Maps and posters of vacation spots to help generate ideas.

Procedures
- At the conclusion of a unit on transportation, discuss advantages and disadvantages of a variety of modes of travel. Brainstorm destinations for trips the students have taken or would like to take. Have students select a destination for a week long vacation trip. Direct students to write a description of their real or imaginary trip being sure to include references to types of transportation used throughout the trip.

Modifications
- Imaginary trips could involve historical time settings or foreign lands.
- Provide students with a list of less common modes of transportation—for example, kayak, hydrofoil, the Concorde, cog railroad, etc.—and ask them to develop a fictional trip that would appropriately fit the means of transportation chosen.

32. ECONOMIC CONCEPTS

Objectives
- Identify the difference between something that is a "want" and something that is a "need."

Materials
- *Children's Writing and Publishing* program.

Procedures
- Brainstorm a list of things people spend money for.
- Discuss the concept of needs and wants, and the difference between them.

- Return to the list of brainstormed items and code them as wants or needs. Discuss the possibility of an item's being either depending on the situation.

- Using the computer program, select the newsletter format so that there are two columns. Label one column "Wants" and the other "Needs."

- Have students fill in the columns with a list of their own wants and needs.

- Working in cooperative groups, analyze each other's lists and determine whether items listed really fit the definition of needs.

Modifications
- Analyze the role of advertising in creating the feeling of need.

- Explore the relationship between the law of supply and demand in the creation of wants and needs.

- Evaluate one's ideas of wants and needs in relationship to the homeless, disaster victims, and the poor.

33. RAW MATERIALS TO FINISHED PRODUCT

Objectives
- Recognize the role of the manufacturing process in transforming raw materials into finished products.

- Sequence steps in the process appropriately.

- Connect raw materials with their finished products.

Materials
- Word processing program.

- Books in the *Start to Finish* series or similar materials.

Procedures
- Discuss where students think certain products come from—for example, leather shoes and belts, glass bottles, fabrics, paper, chalk, pencils, etc.

- Provide each student with a book in the series. As they read, have the students take notes identifying the raw materials and the steps in the manufacturing process.

- Ask the students to write a story from the point of view of the raw materials as they are processed to make the finished product. Ask them to emphasize the experience in terms of what it might feel like.

Modifications
- Create a class book of the writings for sharing.

- Students share their knowledge of their manufacturing process orally with the class.

34. TIMELINE CONSTRUCTION

Objectives
- Interpret chronological order.
- Understand the concept of timeline to convey chronological order.
- Research facts about an author's life.

Materials
- *Timeliner* program.
- Reference works such as *Something About the Author* or other suitable biographical references.

Procedures
- Review attributes of chronological order and biographical information.
- Students select an author and locate pertinent information to use in the timeline.
- Demonstrate the *Timeliner* program.
- Students create a timeline by using the computer program.

Modifications
- Analyze timelines to put authors into historical context. What major historical events were taking place when the author was alive?
- Use the merge function of the *Timeliner* program to create a composite for authors who were contemporaries.

35. IMPACT OF GEOGRAPHY ON LIFE

Objectives
- Identify the relationship between patterns of daily life and geographic conditions.
- Utilize cause and effect reasoning.
- Utilize descriptive vocabulary.

Materials
- Word processing program.
- Appropriate materials throughout the unit to provide background knowledge.

Procedures
- Provide opportunities for students to research regional differences (Eastern woodland, Plains, Northwestern, and Southwestern) in food, clothing, shelter, weapons, and crafts used by Native Americans.
- Having students construct a web or chart to record their findings.
- Working from their web or chart ask students to agree or disagree with the following statement: Where individuals lived determined the skills

they learned. Include specific examples of how Native Americans' daily life was affected by physical geography and natural resources.

Modifications
- Varying criteria such as the specific number of examples to include from each region could be given as a means of providing differentiation.

36. NEWSPAPER RECRUITMENT AD

Objectives
- Apply techniques of persuasion.
- Identify key features of specific voyages of exploration.
- Apply writing style appropriate for purpose—for example, that of a classified advertisement.

Materials
- Word processing program.

Procedures
- Brainstorm examples of exploration throughout history.
- Discuss common theme of going into the unknown.
- Have students select an explorer and his goal to research.
- Ask students to create a classified ad for a newspaper designed to recruit crew members for the trip. Include name of the explorer, destination, skills needed, possible personal rewards (if successful), and references to conditions during the trip.

Modifications
- Printed copies of finished ads could be compiled into a "newspaper" and posted on a bulletin board. Students could read them and determine which were most persuasive and why.
- Real and or imaginary explorations could be incorporated depending on the purpose—writing persuasion or assessing content related to unit on early explorers.
- Ask students to imagine that they are crew members on a voyage of exploration. Have them write a letter home describing their experiences making sure they include such topics as strange sights they have seen, weather conditions experienced, and their thoughts and feelings.
- Be prepared to deal with students placing 800 phone numbers in their classified ads, and the fact that the explorers would have had to send their letters home with other travellers (should they encounter any) due to lack of postal services. Neither point is an obstacle to the writing experience, but the teacher might want to discuss such technological misplacements with the class.

37. LETTERS TO THE FAMILY

Objectives
- Write using the appropriate letter format.
- Determine what information could be shared with others and what might need to be kept confidential.
- Emphasize the impact of historical events on participants' lives.

Materials
- Word processing program.
- Primary and secondary reference materials on historical topics.

Procedures
- Share samples of letters and diaries written by historical figures as examples of primary source documents.
- Discuss the types of information included in them emphasizing impact of events on pattern of daily life.
- Ask students to create a web of incidents and feelings related to an historical event chosen. Choose from the following events in Colonial history: The first Thanksgiving of the Pilgrim Settlers, signing of the Declaration of Independence, surrender at Yorktown, purchasng of Manhattan from the Indians, and the Constitutional Convention in Philadelphia.
- Write a letter to family or friends telling, from your point of view, what is happening around and to you during the event chosen.

Modifications
- Similar activities could be designed for other periods in American history or world history.
- Write a letter from one historical figure to another contemporary figure trying to persuade him or her to adopt your point of view.

38. OCCUPATIONS

Objectives
- Build generalizations based on specific details. Recognize that basic human needs tend to remain constant when technology is used to meet changes.
- Categorize occupations by needs met.

Materials
- Word processing program.
- Chart paper and markers for making lists.

Procedures
- Working in cooperative groups, have students in some groups brainstorm lists of Colonial occupations as students in other groups brainstorm modern day occupations.
- Post the lists and let the total group make adjustments to the lists.
- Categorize and group Colonial occupations; categorize and group modern occupations.
- Moving to the computer lab, ask students to write observations identifying similarities and differences in specific occupations and categories developed during previous class discussion.
- Share writings and discuss relationships identified.

Modifications
- Select a Colonial period job and look for its modern day counterpart. Look for evidence of the impact of changing technology in such trades as blacksmith and automobile mechanic.
- Have the whole group discuss the topic first and write a follow-up to show understanding of concepts.

39. FOUNDING FATHERS

Objectives
- Identify contributions of the Founding Fathers in forming the new nation.

Materials
- Word processing program.

Procedures
- At the end of a unit on the formation of the new nation, and as a part of evaluation, ask the students to summarize the contributions of each of the following Founding Fathers: John Adams, Benjamin Franklin, Alexander Hamilton, Patrick Henry, John Jay, Thomas Jefferson, James Madison, and George Washington.

Modifications
- Have students select an additional person and justify why he should be included as a Founding Father.
- Discuss why they think all of the recognized founders were men.

40. REASONS FOR WESTWARD MOVEMENT

Objectives
- Identify reasons causing people to go West.
- Categorize reasons in terms of those pushing people out of the East and those which attracted or pulled them West.

Materials
- *Children's Writing and Publishing* program.
- Appropriate resource materials to determine causes of the Westward Movement.

Procedures
- Generate a list of reasons for going West.
- Categorize reasons according to whether they were pushing people out of the East or pulling them to the West.
- Using *Children's Writing and Publishing*, select Newsletter format, with heading. In heading section select an appropriate graphic and use the title: Causes for the Westward Movement.
- Label the first column "Push" and the second column "Pull." List factors influencing families and individuals to move West in the appropriate column.
- Compare lists and discuss discrepancies in placement of factors.

Modifications
- Any major influx of immigration to the United States could be analyzed in the same manner—for example the Potato Famine in Ireland, the War in El Salvador, the poverty in Mexico, and the new freedoms in Eastern Europe.

41. TRAILS WEST

Objectives
- Locate on a map the major routes to the West such as the Oregon Trail, the Santa Fe Trail, etc.
- Identify the conditions of daily life on the trail, and differences in weather conditions and terrain travellers would have encountered.

Materials
- *Timeliner*.
- Appropriate materials for researching trail conditions and typical happenings.

Procedures
- Have students read and view materials to gain background information about the events that occurred during wagon train trips West.
- Using *Timeliner*, have students create a timeline for an imaginary trip following one of the major trails. The initial entry would be the date and place of departure and the final entry would be date and location of arrival at destination. Have students include a minimum of twenty entries incorporating events related to geographical features such as river crossings, mountain passes, sources of drinking water; and events of human interest such as births, deaths, celebrations, encounters with

Indians or wild animals etc. Encourage students to demonstrate a plausible elapsed time for the trip.

Modifications

- Timelines could be prepared by cooperative groups rather than by individual students.
- Additional settings could be used such as the Pony Express Route, or a round trip on the Natchez Trace.

42. CONFLICTS IN LAND USE

Objectives

- Identify the major acquisitions of land that form the present boundaries of the United States.
- Identify who settled those areas as they were opened up and sources of conflict among various groups of users.

Materials

- Word processing program.
- Appropriate reference materials to support the unit.

Procedures

- Identify on a map the areas included in the major land purchases that opened up the West—for example, the Louisiana Purchase.
- Discuss geographical features of these land areas.
- Discuss who settled these areas and how they made a living.
- Identify conflicting interests and the nature of the conflicts.
- Have students select one of the pairs and write a description of the differences in philosophies of land use. Include explanations of the causes of potential conflict. Sample pairs: Trappers and Native Americans, or ranchers and farmers.

Modifications

- Create other pairs in conflict in our own times and analyze them for sources of conflicts—for example, conservationists and lumber industry, private profit from public wilderness areas, landfills and waste management issues.

43. FAMILY'S FIRST AMERICAN

Objectives

- Identify the member of your family who first immigrated to the United States.
- Understand the concept of the United States as a "melting pot."

- Recognize relationships identified by terms used for family members—for example, aunt, uncle, cousin, or great grandparent.
- Have each student identify his or her relationship to the family's first American.

Materials
- Word processing program.
- Examples of antique photographs or realia that would be reminiscent of past generations.

Procedures
- Use the photographs and realia to spark a discussion about students' ancestors.
- Let students share what they know about the origins of their families. Explain that the students will be writing a description of their family's "First American."
- Have students find out necessary information: Who the person was; where that person came from; when he or she came, and why; and some experiences in coming to America.
- Have students write and revise their pieces.

Modifications
- Plot on a map or create a bar graph showing distribution of ethnic backgrounds represented in the class.
- Match the arrivals of classroom ancestors with major immigration trends, and events that pushed them out of homelands.
- Share stories during an international evening with parents.

44. IMPACT OF INDUSTRIAL REVOLUTION

Objectives
- Define the concept of mass production and assembly lines.
- Identify causes of the Industrial Revolution.
- Recognize the impact of changing manufacturing processes on daily life.

Materials
- Word processing program.
- Appropriate materials to support research on the Industrial Revolution.

Procedures
- Divide the class in half. Provide each group with raw materials for producing the same number of finished products.

- Have the students in one group work individually to produce the product from start to finish. Have the other group utilize the assembly line concept where each student performs a portion of the total process.
- Provide the same amount of time for each group so that an assessment can be made regarding the number and quality of finished products.
- Based on their experience, have the students describe, in writing, the advantages and disadvantages of mass production using an assembly line.

Modifications
- Students could research products that were early adapters in the change to mass production.
- Discuss whether there is a place for handwork in modern manufacturing—for example, hand decorating of china, Steuben glass, weaving, etc.

45. ANCIENT GREEK JOB DESCRIPTIONS

Objectives
- Analyze the advantages and disadvantages of various positions in ancient Greek society.
- Recognize the elements of a job description.

Materials
- Word processing program.
- Appropriate resources for unit of study.

Procedures
- During the unit of study discuss results on daily life of being born into various positions.
- As part of culminating activities ask students to write job descriptions for selected positions from a list. Included in each job description should be indication of responsibilities and privileges, as well as skills or talents required by individuals serving in each position.
- List of jobs: Politician, playwright, astronomer, teacher, wealthy boy, slave, architect, sculptor, farmer, actor, scientist, messenger [runner], and trading ship crew member.

Modifications
- Specific positions could be required of all students and choice be included for additional examples.
- The total number of job descriptions to be completed could be adjusted to fit needs of students.

46. SIMILAR BUT DIFFERENT

Objectives

- Define vocabulary introduced in unit on Ancient Greece.
- Identify relationships between related terms.

Materials

- Word processing program.
- Appropriate research materials for use during the unit of study.

Procedures:

- During discussion throughout the unit of study introduce terms in context. Provide experiences during discussions to identify relationships, similarities, and differences among various terms.
- As part of the end of unit assessment, ask students to explain as clearly as possible the differences between the pairs of terms listed.
- Paired terms list: Stadium and amphitheater, Doric and Ionic, temple and oracle, Sparta and Athens, shopkeeper and craftsman, playwright and poet, scientist and mathematician, education for boys and for girls, tunic and toga, and the Acropolis and the Parthenon.

Modifications

- Specific word pairs could be required for all students while other pairs provide an element of choice.
- Students could be asked to create additional word pairs of their own to use.

47. ANIMALS: ZOO, FARM, AND OCEAN

Objectives

- Grasp the concepts of zoo, farm, and ocean as habitats for animals.
- Categorize animals according to habitats.
- Recognize that for some animals placement in more than one category could be defended—for example, ostriches and buffalo would be considered by many people as zoo animals but they are now raised on farms for meat; seals, which live in the ocean, are exhibited at zoos.

Materials

- Word processing program.

Procedures

- Brainstorm animals that live in a zoo to define concept of a zoo as a habitat.
- Have students type the heading "Zoo Animals" and direct them to begin making a list of animals that live in a zoo.

- Encourage them to think of additional examples when they first stall.
- Direct the students to stroke return two or three times to space down the page and enter the new heading "Farm Animals."
- Students are then directed to generate a list of farm animals.
- The procedure is repeated for "Ocean Animals."
- Save and/or print out the lists.

Modifications

- Share lists to verify that animals listed fit the category.
- Share lists to discover additional animals that fit each category.
- Select an animal from a list and find out about it.
- Create group collages showing animals in their habitats.
- Look for overlaps to discover animals that could fit more than one category depending on circumstances. For example, seals live in the ocean but also appear in zoos, or an ostrich that is a zoo animal in most places can be a farm animal in others (experimental U.S. farms.)
- This activity is designed for students with limited keyboarding skills. Having younger students write in a list format generates more information than sentences and paragraphs because of keyboarding obstacle. Although being able to write in complete sentences is a priority skill, there are times when alternate formats are advantageous.

48. THE IMPORTANT THING ABOUT WINTER

Objectives

- Identify main idea and supporting details.
- Generate list of attributes of winter.
- Follow a pattern.

Materials

- Word processing program.
- Copy of the book *The Important Book* by Margaret Wise Brown. An LCD.

Procedures

- Read the story to the students asking them to listen for the pattern.
- Discuss the pattern pointing out that there is a main idea followed by supporting details with the main idea being repeated at the end.
- Have students use the pattern to write about winter.
- Use the LCD to project the pattern with the beginning sentence: The important thing about winter is ... Have the students copy this prompt and go on to complete their pattern passages.

- Ask students to proofread their work and make sure that they are following the pattern; save and print.

Modifications
- Students can illustrate their printout.
- Finished pages can be bound into a class book. Or students could select an object and apply the pattern writing about it.
- These pages could be bound together to create a class "Important Book."

49. SEASONAL DESCRIPTIONS

Objectives
- Categorize attributes of the seasons.
- Use adjectives to create a seasonal description.
- Generate text which creates mental pictures.

Materials
- Word processing program.
- Pictures of seasonal landscapes.

Procedures
- Discuss the pictures identifying clues which depict a specific season.
- Brainstorm lists of words that are climatic indicators, traditional activities, types of clothing, holidays, etc., for each of the four seasons experienced in the temperate zones.
- Have students create a verbal snapshot incorporating sufficient clues in order that other students can readily identify the season being described.

Modifications
- Take the same setting and describe it in the sequence of the seasons.
- Have students draw a picture to illustrate their passage.
- Display the pictures and have the teacher read a description.
- Have the students identify the picture that matches.
- Discuss which is more distinctive—the written or pictorial descriptions.

50. LIFE CYCLE OF A BUTTERFLY

Objectives
- Apply the concept of a life cycle.
- Sequence correctly the stages of the butterfly's life cycle.
- Use the specialized vocabulary that applies.

Materials
- Word processing program.

Procedures
- Students had already watched the transformation of butterflies from eggs to adults in their classroom making this project a culminating event.
- The project was spread over two writing periods.
- In the first session terminology referring to the egg and larvae stages was reviewed.
- After the brief verbal review, students wrote from the point of view of a butterfly of their experiences as an egg and a larvae.
- The text was saved and called up for continuing in the second session.
- During the second session, terminology related to the pupae and adult stages was reviewed prior to having the students write.
- Revision and editing was done before printing out the final copies.
- Students were evaluated on their factual accuracy and the terminology was incorporated into their writing.

Modifications
- Students' written explanations of the life cycle demonstrated that they had acquired the real meaning for the scientific terms and functions of body parts they had been observing.
- Individual students had their own butterflies. (All were Painted Ladies). A releasing ceremony was held when the adult butterflies were let go on the school grounds.

51. LETTERS TO BUTTERFLIES

Objectives
- Use correct form for personal letters.

Materials
- Word processing program.

Procedures
- Shortly after releasing the butterflies used in a science unit, the form for writing letters was introduced.
- To practice using the form, students wrote letters to their recently released butterflies.
- The placements of the date and greeting were done as a group.
- The text of the letter was generated by individual students.
- The closing was, again, done as a group to ensure proper placement.

Modifications
- Although the butterflies would not be able to answer the students' letters, the students practiced a letter writing form of asking questions that would elicit a response from their correspondents.

- These second graders received a letter from a representative fictitious butterfly (authored by the classroom or library media teacher) responding to questions frequently asked by the students in their letters. Although the students know rationally that this cannot happen, it does extend the pleasure of the letter writing process.

52. KITES

Objectives
- Categorize according to the five senses.
- Recognize kites as a symbol of spring.
- Work on an extended (3 weeks) project.
- Experience flying a kite.

Materials
- Word processing program.
- Assorted kites.

Procedures
- Give the students the experience of flying a kite.
- Talk about the variation of perspective depending upon which end of the kite string you are looking from.
- Discuss what a kite might be seeing, hearing, and feeling as it flies in the air. Fears as well as exaltation should be included.
- Initiate the writing experience by having all of the students type the following prompt: I am a kite up in the air. Looking down I see ... and have the students respond by describing what the kite might see from its perspective in the air.
- During the second writing session call up the previous file and add the following prompt: I am a kite up in the air. I hear ...
- During the third writing session call up the previous file and add on the prompt: I am a kite up in the air. I feel ...
- Revise, edit as desired, and at the conclusion of this session print out the complete document.

Modifications
- Take the point of view of some other inanimate object's perspective such as a rock, a postage stamp on a letter, a box of cereal on the shelf, picture hanging on a wall, etc.

53. WEATHER FORECAST

Objectives
- Identify components of weather forecasts.
- Categorize weather conditions according to seasons.

- Expand vocabulary related to describing weather conditions.
- Think through reasons for liking or disliking kinds of weather.

Materials
- Word processing program.
- Pictures of various weather conditions.
- Recorded samples of TV or radio weather forecasts or newspaper forecasts.

Procedures
- Discuss a number of different weather conditions.
- Discuss components of a weather forecast.
- Analyze sample weather forecasts for information that is included.
- Examine vocabulary used.
- Choose the type of weather you like best—for example, a sunny day at the beach, a crisp fall afternoon, or a winter blizzard.
- Write a description of your favorite type of day, and write a weather forecast for it. Include details about temperature, precipitation, and wind.

Modifications
- Examine the tools used by meteorologists.
- Explore the natural phenomena which create disasters and look for related weather factors such as hurricanes, tornados, blizzards, forest fires, etc.

54. ALPHABET OF FACTS

Objectives
- Apply background knowledge on a topic.
- Develop ability to reword concepts to meet specific criteria.
- Play with words to create phrases for difficult letters.
- Use research skills to find needed facts.

Materials
- Word processing program.
- Reference or nonfiction collection.

Procedures
- Provide an example of an alphabet of facts—for example, for the topic of *Frogs*, facts might include "Amphibians live part of their lives in water and part on land," "Big bulging eyes," ... "Jelly protects eggs," ... or "Tadpoles have two rows of tiny teeth," etc.

- Select a topic of student's choice.
- Generate a phrase or fact related to your topic that starts with each letter of the alphabet.
- Sequence facts in alphabetical order.
- Research facts for missing letter representations.

Modifications
- Learn to use different fonts to print distinctive (larger, fancier, or thematic) alphabet letters different from their accompanying facts text.
- Use the facts as a source of ideas.
- Create a poem by using the following format: First line a noun, second line three descriptors, third line two actions, and fourth line a synonym to the first line.

55. ACTION CONTRAPTION

Objectives
- Interpret advertising techniques to recognize the manipulation of potential purchasers.
- Create a contraption to serve a practical or imaginary purpose.
- Apply techniques of persuasive writing.

Materials
- Collection of reusable items such as boxes, paper towel tubes, juice cans, non-glass containers, spools, construction toy pieces such as Legos, etc.
- Construction paper, glue, markers, string, tape, scissors, etc.
- Word processing program.

Procedures
- Working at home, or in the classroom, make an action contraption.
- Discuss advertising techniques and persuasive writing.
- Write an advertisement explaining what your contraption can do. Make sure you include a name, address, selling price, and why someone would want to purchase your product.

Modifications
- Hold an action contraption sales convention and invite other classes to view the contraptions and advertisements.
- Invite parents to view them, too.
- Students should be on hand to explain and answer questions.

56. ANIMAL HABITATS

Objectives
- Establish the concept of habitat.
- Identify the characteristics of each habitat—for example, tundra, desert, rainforest, grasslands, woodland, fresh water pond, tidepool, seashore.
- Differentiate among a variety of habitats noting similarities and differences.

Materials
- Word processing program.

Procedures
- At the conclusion of a study of the relationship between animals and their habitats, evaluate student understanding by having them write.
- For each of the habitats identified by the teacher, the student will write a paragraph including an animal that lives there, the materials provided for shelter, food sources, and necessary water to support that animal's life.

Modifications
- Rather than using the project as evaluation, the student could have one habitat to research and write about during the unit.
- Research could include additional components such as multiple animals living in the habitat, adaptations they have made, predators and other dangers they face.
- The influence of man on the habitat could be explored.

57. ANIMAL RELATED TERMS

Objectives
- Expand vocabulary; differentiate between pairs of words.

Materials
- Word processing program.

Procedures
- Verify understanding of the vocabulary introduced during an animal unit by asking students to explain, in writing, the difference between the following pairs of words: Migration and metamorphosis, sleep and hibernation, regeneration and reproduction, fur and feathers, vertebrate and invertebrate, aquatic and amphibian, cold blooded and warm blooded, photosynthesis and digestion, intelligence and instinct, endangered and extinct, etc.

Modifications
- Included in the student's writing could be identifying animals that fit each category.
- Ask students to list additional pairs of scientific terms that could be easily confused—for example, weather and climate, condensation and evaporation, convex and concave, hurricanes and tornadoes.

58. WATER CYCLE

Objectives
- Develop concept of "cycle" as being unending.
- Define terminology related to the water cycle.

Materials
- Word processing program.
- Diagram of the water cycle.

Procedures
- At the conclusion of a unit of study which would have included hands on experiments such as making clouds rain, condensation and evaporation, etc., ask students to write a description following a drop of water through the water cycle. Remind them to include all of the steps and to use correct vocabulary.
- Printed passages should be printed out and handed in for evaluation.

Modifications
- Carry out some demonstrations involving water such as changing it from water to steam, or to ice and back to water.
- Examine other cycles in the natural world such as food chains, life cycles, phases of the moon, tides, seasons, and patterns of night and day.

59. FOOD PAIRS

Objectives
- Identify similarities and differences.

Materials
- Word processing program.

Procedures
- Provide students with a list of pairs of words related to foods—for example, beef stew and vegetable soup, meatloaf and sausage, apple and orange, tomato and watermelon, rice and corn, pretzels and potato chips, cookies and crackers.
- As a prewriting activity, have students create a Venn diagram listing similarities and differences for the pair. Discuss attributes which could be

similar or different such as shape, color, texture, structure, taste, ingredients, processed or natural, etc.

- Use the diagram as a source of information to write a paragraph describing the two foods, emphasizing their similarities and differences.

Modifications
- Have a tasting party to observe details overlooked in the writing.
- Have the party before writing if new foods are being introduced.
- Have the party after writing to observe details that may have been overlooked.
- Nutritional similarities and differences can be investigated for the pairs of foods written about.

60. INFLUENCE OF TECHNOLOGY

Objectives
- Recognize influence of technology on daily life; identify the connection between inventing and problem solving.

Materials
- Word processing program.

Procedures
- Working in cooperative groups, develop webs that show various ways inventions have influenced daily life. Assign each group a different invention such as television, computer, airplane, automobile, sewing machine, or refrigeration.
- Post the webs and discuss them with the whole class, making additions and deletions as necessary.
- Have each student select the invention he or she thinks is the most influential and write an explanation justifying that choice.

Modifications
- Expand the list of inventions to be considered; focus on a specific time period or ethnic group.
- Research the inventor and identify the motivation behind the invention—for example, Eastman, not wanting to cart around so much equipment to take pictures, invented film; Howe, wanting to make it possible for his wife to sew more easily, invented the sewing machine.

61. TECHNOLOGY, FRIEND OR FOE?

Objectives
- Recognize the role technology has played in helping people control nature.

- Recognize the negative affects of technology on the planet.
- Use specific examples to build a logical argument for one point of view.

Materials
- Word processing program.
- Appropriate reference materials to build arguments.

Procedures
- At the end of a unit on technology, ask which has had the greater impact on human life, the advantages or disadvantages of technology. Have students write a description of their position and defend it by using examples from throughout history.

Modifications
- Limit choices of inventions to specific time periods, types of inventions, or geographic areas.
- Have students look into the future and predict whether technology will be a friend or foe.
- Students could use their research for the written piece as material for a debate.

8
EVALUATION OF STUDENT PROJECTS

Changing emphases and patterns of instruction has an impact on the nature of writing assignments and their assessment. "Choosing topics. Researching. Composing rough drafts. Conferencing with peers. It's the day-to-day work of today's writing classroom. This new kind of writing work demands that students exhibit complex behaviors that focus on process, encourage reflection, and promote self-knowledge—complex behaviors that yesterday's evaluation techniques don't address. Fortunately, teachers across the country are designing new tools for observing, tracking, and reporting student progress in the writing classroom."[1]

Assessment of writing is more than looking at the finished product. It is essential to evaluate the *writing process*, and this is a responsibility of both the teacher and the student. Each has a unique role. The teacher uses observation as a form of evaluation. The teacher "wants to look for sharing, initiating, risk taking, questioning, revising, goal setting, collaboration, inventive spelling, choosing/developing topics, editing, and brainstorming."[2] What has happened to looking for spelling, grammar, punctuation, and neatness of writing? It still enters into the picture, but is the final step after ideas have been developed, sequenced, organized, and drafted. The focus is shifting to placing priority on the quality of the *content*, of the ideas expressed. However, it is equally important to convey to the student the ultimate necessity of following conventions of spelling, grammar, and punctuation if ideas are to be communicated.

Furthermore, in the real world, much writing is done in a collaborative environment. The schools need to reflect the work place where many projects are assigned to teams and solutions are the result of their verbal and written interactions. Working in this way requires goal setting, brainstorming, questioning, giving suggestions, risk taking, and revising. All of these require collaborative activity. Writing assessments which ask the student to sit and write for a specified time, on a given topic, turning in a finished product at the end of the session are not a valid assessment of the writing process. While this format permits assessment of the mechanics (spelling, grammar, punctuation), it does not provide the student with an authentic writing situation. There is no time to let ideas percolate, to go back and read the draft cold to assess its ability to communicate. In this format, little revision occurs; basically, an initial draft is recopied with some proofreading corrections having been made.

An emerging alternative form of assessing writing is the use of writing folders or portfolios. "Among the options for alternative assessment strategies that break away from traditional measures, none has captured the imagination more than portfolio assessment. Extrapolated from 'artists' portfolios, the assessment strategy attempts to provide extended records of student performance, to motivate students to choose and reflect on their efforts, and to provide an occasion for teacher-student classroom instruction, all outcomes in short supply in the typical classroom experience. ... Portfolios change the character of instructional interaction and contribute to learning. The challenge with portfolios comes when we attempt to use them as formal measures of educational change."[3]

Individuals interested in using this approach to assessment need to provide each student with a writing folder. Students keep all materials related to a writing project in this folder. Webs, lists, all prewriting material, initial drafts, and revisions remain available. It is helpful to label papers as "draft," "revision," "editing" so that students know where they are in the process. Rubber stamps are one way of managing this process.

It is essential that students learn self-evaluation techniques and are given time regularly to reflect on and judge their own writing progress. To help with this, a second set of folders becomes a storage place for selected writing samples. One format for creating a final presentation portfolio is to have the student provide a table of contents, pick a best piece, write a letter about the best piece to the teacher that explains how the best piece was chosen, and the process the student followed to produce the final draft; include a poem, short story, play, or personal narration; a personal response to a cultural media or sports event, or book, current event, math problem, or scientific phenomenon; a prose piece from any subject area other than English.[4] This five item "showcase" portfolio is used to document types of writing experiences that the student has been exposed to.

Another self-evaluation technique is to have students take a self-evaluation inventory at the beginning of each month or marking period. Ask students "What skills are you trying to learn right now?" "What writing skills are you best at?" "What type of writing do you enjoy most?" Ask students to jot down in their journals one thing they learned, accomplished, or attempted during the period, such as "I learned to use a colon correctly today," and to write a single goal for the next workshop.[5]

Concern is expressed by individuals attempting to document growth in writing through the use of portfolios when they are trying to compare different genres. "A portfolio mix of genres obscures evidence of change over time in writing quality. Comparing an October folktale with a December fantasy, a

January haiku, a March whale report, a May letter to a penpal, and a June summary of a field trip was an impossible task."[6] In terms of assessing writing, there are commonalities in the process whether the piece is a poem, a story, or a report. "The most effective evaluations are those that take place while students are actually engaged in writing." [7] This form of assessment is effective because it focuses on the commonalities of the writing process which need to be applied across genre. Although there are specific attributes related to individual genre such as poems, fables, myths, etc., there is an underlying core of attributes of good writing common to all. It is this core that is used to measure growth in writing.

One approach to organizing these core attributes of writing for the purpose of assessment has been done by the National Center for Research on Evaluation, Standards, and Student Testing. They created an *Elementary Narrative Holistic/Analytic Scale* which described six levels of writing proficiency. In this scale, attention is focused on indicators of Focus/Organization, Development, and Mechanics.

A Level 1, Insufficient Writer, shows minimal evidence of achievement. The topic is not clear, lacks an organizational plan, is filled with digressions or elaborations, has few or no transitions, almost no sense of beginning and end; no development of narrative elements, no details, incomplete sentence patterns; many major and minor mechanical errors causing reader confusion and difficulty in reading.

A Level 2, Emerging Writer, shows limited evidence of achievement. The topic may not be clear, few events are logical, much digression and over elaboration with significant interference with reader understanding, few transitions, little sense of beginning and end; minimal development of elements of narration, detail used is uneven and unclear, simple sentence patterns, simplistic vocabulary, details may be irrelevant or confusing; many major and minor errors cause reader confusion and interfere with understanding.

A Level 3, Developing Writer, shows some evidence of achievement. The topic is clear, most events are logical, some digression or over elaboration interfere with reader understanding, begins to use transitions, limited sense of beginning and end; elements of narration are not evenly developed, vocabulary not appropriate at times, some supporting details may be present; some major and minor errors cause reader confusion.

A Level 4, Adequate Writer. The topic is clear, most events are logical, some digression causing slight reader confusion, most transitions are logical but may be repetitive, clear sense of beginning and end; most elements of narration are present, some elaboration may lack depth, some details are vivid and specific, supporting details begin to be more specific than general statements; few major or minor errors do not cause significant reader confusion.

A Level 5, Commendable Writer. The topic is clear and events are logical, possible slight digression without significant distraction to reader, most transitions are smooth and logical, clear sense of beginning and end; elements of narrative are evenly and appropriately elaborated, some varied sentence patterns and appropriate vocabulary used, some details are more vivid or specific than general statements; few minor errors, one or two major errors which do not cause significant reader confusion.

A Level 6, Excellent Writer. The topic is clear, events are logical, no digressions; transitions are smooth, logical, and varied, clear sense of beginning and end; even and appropriate elaboration of elements of narration, complex and varied sentence patterns, details are vivid and specific; one or two minor errors with no major errors.[8]

It is the intent of instruction to help students progress through these levels of writing. Within any classroom there will be students functioning at a range of levels. For this reason, it is important to begin to provide writing experiences for the very young. "We never discover what children can do if we don't allow them to show us. Young children can write. Two, three, and four year olds can and should write. When children are given the opportunities to read and write in a developmental kindergarten, those children who are ready will begin to write." [9] Once students recognize the connection between speaking, writing, and reading, they move easily from one form of communication to another. Their interest in words as the way of sharing meaning increases. "If sentences are the structures which carry the child's meaning, then words are the bricks within these structures. Part of any successful writing program must be the development of the child's interest in words and a delight in using them. This does not mean that the teacher has to find time within an overloaded curriculum for vocabulary lessons. It asks that the teacher recognizes that all subject areas will provide opportunities for discussing the way in which words are used within them. What the teacher should aim to provide is a word-rich climate within the classroom."[10]

Prereaders who are beginning to write need to be encouraged to express their ideas in writing without being restrained by the need to spell correctly. This results in their using "invented spelling." "To decipher young children's writing, it is necessary to understand what invented spelling is. Read discovered that young children spell words similarly and in a way that makes sense, although adults may have a difficult time understanding the spellings. Young children spell very closely to the way sounds are actually made."[11] Students need to learn to spell in the context of meaningful writing rather than by memorizing an isolated list of words each week. "The teaching of spelling should always be kept in perspective. Spelling is not a 'basic skill' in writing. It is always of secondary importance to the child's effective communication of something that is worth communicating. The basic skills in writing are always the composing skills, not the 'secretarial skills' of spelling and handwriting."[12] There have been studies made which analyze children's writing for creating a lexicon of most frequently used words and the patterns of spelling errors these children use. In one instance a list of 500 words was identified which constituted over half of those used in children's writing. The correlation between these words and the traditional spelling and comprehension lists is minimal. Numerous word changes reflect the cultural changes that have taken place in society.

One of the effects of the Whole Language approach has been to integrate writing throughout the curriculum. Writing assignments designed to assess comprehension in content areas such as social studies, science, and math have formed a bridge with the thinking skills movement. In a report on the National Assessment of Educational Progress (1988), it is stated that "Writing has the potential to foster deeper and more critical thinking about what a student has read. When students are asked to analyze, interpret or evaluate what they have read (and to do so in writing), they must not only reason effectively, but must also communicate their ideas in ways that others can understand. This sort of critical thinking is often perceived to be at the heart of an academic education."[13] Whatever the form of the student's final product—written, oral, filmed—the criteria that will be used to evaluate its success by either peers or teachers will be based on criteria derived from elements of higher order thinking. How many, and how well, thinking strategies were applied becomes apparent in the student's presentation. Students should be helped to recognize what higher order thinking skills are considered to be, and they should be encouraged to become self-conscious about their own thinking and work to develop self-monitoring problem-solving strategies. This applies to students of all levels of capability. "Two of the challenges parents and educators of gifted students have faced is to find ways to help them be critical thinkers and problem solvers and to provide them with activities which challenge and develop their higher order thinking skills."[14]

To help accomplish these ends, there is a nationally recognized staff development program (known as McRAT) designed to help teachers infuse higher order thinking skills and multicultural concepts into the existing curriculum. In their literature the following definition of higher order thinking is given: Students engage in purposeful, extended lines of thought during which they identify the task or problem type, define and clarify essential elements and terms, judge and connect relevant information, evaluate the adequacy of information and procedures for drawing conclusions and/or solving problems. Commonly specified higher order reasoning processes are: 1. Cognitive—ability to analyze, compare, infer or interpret, and evaluate; 2. Metacognitive—plan, monitor, review or revise.[15]

The role of the teacher in teaching writing is becoming increasingly recognized. There is great skill required to help students move beyond the structure of writing. When students learn spelling and sentence structure they are learning rules and the way things are done. They follow or imitate the established patterns. "But when they develop arguments, conduct research, or solve problems such imitation is not only insufficient, it defeats the purpose; we must think for ourselves, as individuals, if we are to write well."[16] Teachers themselves are observing changes in the way they work on writing with their students, and they see their attitudes shifting as they increase their abilities to vary strategies and take greater interest in what students have to say, show less concern over mechanical errors, and contribute to the student's autonomy.

One teacher wondered what her role should be as she moved into a process oriented writing classroom. Would she sit back and observe from a distance, would she wander among groups catching snatches of student discussion and encourage when necessary, or would she engage in modeling and become an active participant? She found that "over time [her] role was defined by the students."[17] She observed and made notes and when she analyzed those notes for her own actions she created a list of nine functions she engaged in. Her first role was to serve as a student's most ardent admirer and astute critic, sometimes simultaneously. She made it her business to see potential in a person and a piece of writing where others might see none.

Second, she helped writers internalize the reader role in order to help communicate intended meaning to others. Students were sometimes surprised that their readers interpreted what they wrote differently than they had anticipated.

Third, she helped students recognize that they were authorities on some topics and had information to share. Tactful, but demanding, questions helped draw out the authors and assisted in their clarifying their thinking. She had to learn to give "wait" time.

Fourth, she protected students as they learned to deal with peer comment. She "read" the student for signs of discomfiture and ameliorated criticism. Peers also had to learn how to phrase their offered comments. She made sure that the student retained ownership of the written piece.

Fifth, she modeled appropriate group responses, questions, and techniques, simultaneously individualizing instruction for the author, using the format of a conference-in-a-group setting, when writing was shared in revision groups.

Sixth, she worked to see that students recognized the tentative state of a draft and saw where their writing was in terms of the total process. She emphasized the value of the improvement resulting from the student's effort, and worked with the student to identify the needed focus in the next draft.

Seventh, she integrated skill instruction within the context of revising writing the student cared about. This could mean providing instruction in mechanics or employment of techniques of description or dialogue, etc. She observed that in this individualized, integrated, and relevant approach students continued to incorporate the skills in their future writing.

Eighth, she monitored individual progress checking to see that the students maintained an identity within the group, approached the group with self-confidence, established ownership of their writing, used suggestions or advice well to improve writing, and learned skills of group interaction.

Ninth, she made sure that she never lost sight of the importance of the human connection. She recognized that students' writing and their selves are one and the same, and that it is the person, often a fragile one, that is the most important factor.[18]

The signifigance of retaining ownership of one's ideas and the written expression of them is exceedingly important. The current emphasis on collaborative work has its place, certainly, but individual creativity and thought must not be lost. As it has been said, "The greatest accomplishments in science and the arts have been made by individuals acting alone. No park has a statue dedicated to a committee."[19]

As teachers discover the power of observing, analyzing and recording children's growth in writing across time, they recognize the value of using these records for planning as well as assessment. "Our desire to have children experiment with language does not reduce our responsibility to evaluate their progress."[20]

One teacher has described an effective way to document the status of an entire class. Each day she notes where each student is in terms of first draft, second draft, editing conference, rewriting final copy, revision conference, self editing, etc. Such charting enables the teacher to be accountable for each student's progress at any point in time."[21]

Means of keeping such notes include the use of a clipboard as the teacher walks around the room observing. The class roster is down the left-hand side of the paper with days of the week across the top. Codes can be used such as w for writing, cf-s for conference with another student, b for brainstorming, ed for editing, etc. These sheets can be filed in a looseleaf notebook along with other notes about students. Another system is to use large cards for making daily notes and file these according to student's names.[22]

They are discovering that students develop skills much earlier than they had believed was possible in the past. As one teacher observes: "I've learned how complex first grade students' thoughts are, and that no matter how young, each student has his or her own philosophy."[23] To nurture the young writers' thoughts and to help develop their means of expressing them, rather than to stifle thought through prescription, is the goal.

Of course, the young child will follow a developmental trail of learning to form letters and recognizing them on a keyboard, of writing from left to right on the line, of the impact of vocabulary, of the effect of increasingly complex sentence structures and paragraphs. At the same time, as they develop their own abilities to think and express their ideas, they will learn to evaluate other people's ideas and to include them in their own arguments. They will shift in Bryson's terms from knowledge telling to knowledge transforming.[24] They will come to "use writing as a central means of learning through discussion and criticism, and all the earlier skills are necessary as part of the more developed education skills."[25]

Parallel to, and necessary for, this type of writing development is the student's own physical and social development. It is necessary for the teacher to recognize the "importance of a clear definition of the task and of the contexts provided for writing in helping a child identify why he is writing and giving him access to details that may support the expression or communication of that purpose. It may be felt that children should be able to do this for themselves. Unfortunately, the child's social environment may not teach him how to meet the demands of writing tasks, especially since they are almost completely school tasks."[26] Children begin organizing their writing as a series of events in time and may "find it difficult to impose shape on static things— for example, the description of a place, person or object....As the child grows older he will increase in his awareness of the otherness of other people. He will appreciate that in some ways they behave as he does but in other ways their behavior will be different. This ability to see an experience from a point of view other than one's own is part of that decentering or disembedding process through which children move. This ability to find meaning in other lives may be put to use in subject areas like history or geography or may enable the child to write sensitively about other human beings whom he encounters."[27]

Asking students to write as if they are historical figures or people from other times and places is likely to be unsuccessful unless the student has sufficient background. "Imagination feeds on knowledge and if a child is to write sympathetically about other lives he has to have some understanding of them; some points of contact should exist."[28] It is for this reason that such an assignment gives insight into what a student may have gained from a unit in history and therefore serve as an evaluative instrument as well as a writing experience. Activities in Chapter 7 such as numbers 32 and 36 use this approach.

In units dealing with scientific content, the student's writing will be less concerned with sensation or emotional response and more with precise physical description or the clear description of process: "This in itself will give the writing a degree of objectivity. The main form of organization can still be chronological as much of the writing will be concerned with observation over time or with the description of processes in time."[29] The student who is unfamiliar with scientific procedure will need guidance in recognizing the need to incorporate statements that let the reader know what they are proposing to do and how they are going to do it as well as closing with a clear summary statement of results, conclusions, applications, or possible further activities. However, "science writing is not dependent on a special language: it is dependent on thinking scientifically; and curiosity, precise observation and a willingness to reflect on data would appear to be more essential than terminology or dependence on a formula for writing."[30]

In evaluating the student's writing, it is necessary to focus attention on the process. When writing is looked at in the context of critical thinking and problem solving, the process becomes more important than the product. In the evaluation of writing as *process*, one "needs to view drafts and revisions as clues to the thinking and writing that go on as the drafts become more and more finished."[31] The final draft product is seen as just one step in the process rather than the only thing that matters.

Evaluating students' writing in this way is a necessary change that is required in response to the shift in ways of teaching thinking skills, writing, and reading in the classroom. Not all classroom and library media teachers have made this shift, but many are moving in the direction of linking content, thinking, and writing in new and effective ways. Many are finding the use of the computer lab an effective tool in bringing greater writing opportunities to their students. It should be remembered that "while there are times when the 'problems' at a school simply can't be solved, almost always what gets in the way is attitude. The believers make it work; the unbelievers make excuses."[32]

APPENDIX

SAMPLE RESPONSES TO CHAPTER 7 WRITING PROMPTS

The following material is intended to be of interest in connection with Chapter 8. Actual student-written examples have been used as illustrations. For this reason, errors have been retained.

The responses are evidence that students' work reflects the levels described in the *Elementary Narrative Holistic/Analytic Scale* on page 83. The examples given are numbered to match the writing prompts found in Chapter 7. In some instances they are arranged from less skilled to more effective products prepared by different students whose abilities vary using the same topic. In other instances, different students respond to a prompt using different topics. In the examples of the revision process the work is done by the same students as they work through drafts and revisions to the finished product. In prompt 47A and the examples of the four intents of writing in prompt 21, the finished products are the work of groups of students writing cooperatively to produce a single product.

Prompt Responses

PROMPT 9. DOORS

Examples illustrate varying abilities of different students using the same topics.

A.

Looking inside the door I see a steering wheel, seats and the other door.

Looking outside the door I see cars and trucks.

B.

Looking inside the door I see a dashboard with dials and gauges. There is a radio and tape player. On the front seat is a map and in the back seat is a child seat and a teddy bear.

Looking outside the door I see other cars and gas pumps. People are waking back with cans of soda and snacks.

C.

Looking inside the door I see jars of pickles, butter tubs, cans of soda and a pitcher of juice. Salad makings and sandwich meats are visible as well. In the middle is a turkey carcass covered with foil.

Looking outside the door I see a sink, counters and a stove. Across the room is a window and a table and chairs. Right next to me is a smelly waste basket.

PROMPT 33. RAW MATERIALS TO FINISHED PRODUCTS

Note: First graders, using the *Start to Finish* series, wrote from the point of view of the raw materials being processed. Peer conferencing provided suggestions for revision of initial drafts. The student's pieces were published using *Newsroom* to allow graphics to be interspersed with text producing a newsletter which was taken home and shared with parents. Examples are by different students using different topics.

A.
Wool to Scarf
Here I am on the sheep's back. One day the shepherd cut me off the sheep, but I will grow back for next winter. Then the shepherd loaded me on a truck and took me to a factory. There I was twisted into balls of yarn. Grandmother buys the yarn and knits winter clothes for next winter.

B.
Grass Becomes Butter
In the faarm there are cows eating fresh green grass. When the cows are old enough they produce milk. That is wehre I come from. I was in the cow's udder and the farmer milked me out of the udder. Then I was pasteurized to kill any disease causing germs and put into a machine called a centrifuge. The centrifuge spins around very fast to separate skim milk from the thick sweet cream. The sweet cream is then put into a butter machine. In this machine the cream is stirred for a long time and finally the butter is formed.

C.
From Cowhide to Shoes
I am a cow. I'm in a meadow. My hide is used to make shoes. First you have to kill me. I don't like bing killed. You also have to take the meat out of me. You

have to take my skin off me. I don't like my skin being pulled off of me. Then my skin is taken to a tannery. They put me into a big machine that spins me around. My skin is soaked in a large barrel of water. It's cold inside. I'm taken out of the barrel. Then I'm cut and stitched and sewn into shoes. Next I go to the store. It's good being new shoes.

PROMPT 47. ANIMALS: ZOO, FARM, AND OCEAN

Note: The following was a modification follow-up in which a group of first graders created, by dictating to their teacher, a single story about cats. In the final product, graphics were inserted throughout the piece. A picture of a cat (computer graphic), the title, date, and contributors' names are given in the heading space.

A.
Cats Know Best

Cats know best how to keep warm by the fireplace. They scratch the rug when they are tired. They sit on beds and sometimes they go to sleep on them. Cats know best how to climb trees. [Picture of tree inserted.] Sometimes birds fly away. Cats jump on to the roof to get them.

Cats know best how to catch mice. They chase them and grab them by the paws and then they eat them. [Picture of mouse.] Cats know best how to eat cat food. People buy it for them. They like fish flavors best.

Cats know best how to play with toys. They like to play with wind-up mice, yarn, and bouncing balls. Cats like to play with jump ropes like a snake. Cats get a lot of exercise running away from dogs and chasing mice.

Cats are good pets. They don't do slobbery licks like dogs. Cats curl up on your lap and purr. Cats sleep on your bed at night. Cats sit on the fence and meow at night. Cats know best how to play nice.

Note: At the end of the year, first grade students read nonfiction animal books and created the following pieces as book reports. They used *Children's Writing and Publishing* program, selected an animal graphic, and published their reports using newsletter format. Examples are by different students using different topics.

B.
Farm Animals

I read a book called Farm Animals and I learned lots of facts. Here are some of them. Chickens are birds who eat grain and other seeds. Hens lay eggs. They sit on the eggs to keep them warm. Cows eat lots of sweet grass. Baby cows are called calves. On hot days pigs roll in the mud. Usually many baby pigs are born at one time.

African Animals

There are many kinds of animals and my book report is about African animals. The lepords spots look like the shadow of leaves. The baby baboon holds on tightly to its mother's fur. Giraffes must be careful when their heads are down because they can not see. The cape buffalo spends most of its time eating grass. On the island the hippos lie down. Elephants squirt water over their backs.

Monarch Butterfly

Each female lays about 300 eggs. The Monarch caterpillar sheds its skin four times. It must hang upside down when it is forming its cocoon. Birds do not eat Monarchs because the caterpillar eats a plant that is poisonous to birds. Monarchs migrate. People were cutting down the trees where the Monarchs live in the winter.

PROMPT 52. KITES

Examples illustrate varying abilities of different students using the same topic.

A.

I am a kite up in the air. Looking down I see people and grass there are houses Cars go by.

I am a kite up in the air. I hear birds and wind.

I am a kite up in the air. I feel cold and alone.

B.

I am a kite up in the air. Looking down I see people who look like ants. Cars and houses look like toys. Off in the distance a lake reflects the sun like a mirror.

I am a kite up in the air. I hear the wind rush by as I sail high. The string sings as it vibrates. Birds chirp and flap their wings all around me. Off in the distance an airplane motor drones on and on.

I am a kite up in the air. I feel happy. The sun shines on me as I float above the trees. Oh no, the wind is dying. Now I am scared. Will I get caught in the tree? Whew I got past that one. Now I can relax.

PROMPT 31. DESCRIPTION OF A TRIP

Examples illustrate varying abilities of different students using the same topic.

A.

Our vacation trip was to go camping for a week. We drove to the park. We rode our bikes around the campground. Once we took a canoe out on the lake. We walked on the trales. Then we drove home.

B.

Last winter we went to Denver to go sking. First we drove to the airport and parked the car. We rode the shuttle bus to the terminal and then boarded the plane. After four hours in the air we landed in Denver. We took the bus to the rental car office and got our car. We drove to the loge and got settled into our room. We were tired so we went to bed soon after dinner. The next morning we took our skis and using the skilift we went up and down the mountain all day. As a special treat we took a ride in the horse drawn sleigh down the snow covered streets of the town. At the end of the week we took drove the rental car back to the airport, flew home and drove our car home. We had lots of fun.

PROMPT 6. MULTIPLE MEANINGS

Note: Responding to a modification, students developed poems using synonyms and antonyms. The structure of the seven line "poem" creates a diamond. Lines one and seven are a word and its antonym. Line two contains two synonyms for the word in line one, and line six contains two synonyms for the word in line seven. Lines three, four, and five include gradations in meaning moving from the first word to the last word. Examples are by different students using different topics.

A.
Giant

Huge, big

Stomping, growing, eating

Oaf, minotaur, * dwarf, elf

Shrinking,

Small, tiny

Midget

B.
Food

Juicy, crunchy

Chewing, frying, eating

Popcorn, ice cream, bread, vegetables

Stinking, disintegrating,

Gross looking

Old, moldy,

Leftovers

C.
Strong

Muscular, Strength,

Working, Slaving, Flexing,

Athlete, Wrestler, Couch Potato, Slob

Eating, Sleeping, Limping,

Wimpy, Lazy,

Weak

PROMPT 12. BURIED TREASURE

Examples illustrate varying abilities of different students using the same topic.

A.

In a hole in my back yard there is a burried treasure. It doesn't mean much to you or me, but to the individual who burried it it could be life or death. Cheekfull by cheekful the little chipmunk buried sunflower seeds under the back step. He would live off his treasure all winter long.

B.

The pirates sailed from island to island looking for the perfect place to bury their treasure. It had to be someplace they could find again or the gold could be lost for ever. Finally they found the right spot. The cove was on the south side of the island. To the east was a distinctive rock formation. The three men loaded the chest of gold coins into the rowboat and headed for the beach. Once ashore they dug a deep hole at the base of the rock. They set the chest in the hole and covered it up. After rowing back to the ship the pirates left the cove. The captian drew a map of the location so they could come back when it was safe and get their treasure.

C.

The outlaw gang studied the route the stage would follow. The trail passed between cliffs five miles outside of town. That was where the hold-up would take place. Friday all their careful planning would pay off. The bank shipment, including the payrole for the mine, was due to arrive on the morning stage. Taking their places behind the bolders the outlaws waited impatiently. Off in the distance the sound began to grow. The horses hoofs and the creaking stage was the focus of their attention. At the last minute the riders appeared in the trail. In a cloud of dust the stage skidded to a stop. Being out manned the driver reluctantly tossed down the cash box. Needing to make a quick get away the outlaws didn't bother to rob the few passengers. They rode off to an abandoned mine shaft and lowered the cashbox into the dark hole. They took a change of shirts out of their saddlebags and quickly changed their appearance. Carefully covering their tracks they rode into town. When they were told about the stage robbery they volunteered to ride with the possy to look for the outlaws.

PROMPT 35. IMPACT OF GEOGRAPHY ON LIFE

Note: These examples resulted from an assignment meant to evaluate students' comprehension of the unit's content. Examples illustrate varying abilities of different students using the same topic.

A.

Native Americans use what was around them. They ate what they could catch and made clothes from skins. Houses were made of sticks or skins or adobe. If it was cold they wore more clothes. They used their feet mostly and some boats of horses to get around. Their life was run by nature.

B.

Native Americans in different places lived differently. Eastern woodland tribes hunted forest game and picked berries for food. Their clothes were made of skins and feathers. Their shelters were made of trees and mud and grasses. In the plains the tribes followed the buffalo. They used it for everything. They ate buffalo meat, used the skin to make tepees and slept under buffalo robes. The tribes that lived in the Southwest made their homes of adobe bricks or caves. They didn't wear much clothes because it was so hot. These tribes ate beans and corn and not so much meat. These differences were due to differences in climate and geography.

C.

Climate and geography determined how the different Native American tribes lived their daily lives. Those living in the Eastern woodlands were surrounded by forests and streams and rivers. They hunted and fished for their food and gathered plants for food and medicine. In the winter they lived in long houses with many families together for warmth and security. In the summer they lived in wigwams and moved around more. Their clothing changed with the seasons as well. Animal skins like deer, rabbit, fox and squirrel were used and decorated with feathers. Canoes were used to travel on the streams and rivers. In contrast the tribes living in the southwest desert had a diffferent lifestyle. They grew crops like corn, beans and squash and depended less on hunting animals for meat to eat. Their homes were made of adobe bricks or built into caves in the cliffs. Pottery was important for making utencils. Water was an important concern for these people. Walking was the main way to get from one place to another before horses were introduced. Between these two extremes lived the Plains tribes. Their daily life revolved around the buffalo heards which grazed on the tall prairie grass. During the nice weather they lived in tepees which could be moved to follow the heards. Before horses were known they used dogs to pull loads of belongings on a travois. In the winter to protect themselves from the cold and winds they lived in earth lodges with sod roofs. They worked hard in the summer to have enough food to make it through the winter. Native Americans used the materials around them for food, clothing, and shelter. Their needs were determined by the climate and habitat they lived in. They developed different skills depending on what they needed to know to survive.

PROMPT 4. BUDDY WRITING

Note: The following story was written after a big snowstorm that had closed schools. In this example the younger student is taking the lead assisted by the older student.

Snow is Fun

Hi my name is Bryan I am talking about how I like snow. I like to make giant snowballs that I jump in. I also like to go down a hill on my belly board. I like to make snowmen, but I jump on them when I finish making them. I like to have snowball fights with my friends, but usually my team wins the snowball fight. I make snowballs and I walk around and I just throw them at people. I also go slieghing down hills with my friends or with my family. I also bury myself in the snow because its fun. I can relax, and I can go to sleep. I like shaking the trees because when I do that the trees drop snow and its funny.

Note: In February, students in kindergarten and grade five worked together on fables with African animals as characters. The older students had been studying fables and the kindergartners had been studying zoo animals.

Royalty Mania

Once upon a time when the world was green, there lived a great lion king named Logan. Logan was very sick and old, so he decided to write out a will. In his will he stated that he wanted all his riches to be spread out evenly among his kingdom and that he wanted Henry Hippo to be the new ruler of Kenya.

But, on a hot summer night, a few days after Logan wrote out his will, he was (according to the legend), killed by the God of Fire for putting out a fire with ice, which was very rare in these times; and not to be used freely. Anyway, Logan was too old and sick, so he died without a fight, and the will was lost forever for Logan was the only one who knew where it was, and Kenya was left without a ruler.

A couple hours later...

Sly Snake, Montie Monkey, Winnie Wasp, Chi Chi Cheeetah, and Eddie Elephant were fighting over who should be King. Then Henry Hippo spoke up, "I have a solution. We could have a contest to see who is worthy to be King."

The contest...

The contestants were ready, all excited and dreaming of castles on hills, riches of gold and jewels; all except one of the contestants anyway. Henry Hippo was only concerned for the welfare of the Kingdom of Kenya. When the contest was over, it was obvious who would be Kenya's new ruler. The bugles blared, the moment of truth finally came. The new ruler of Kenya will be announced in three seconds! "What?!" everyone roared. "Just kidding," a little mosquito said. A large sigh came from the audience. The new ruler of Kenya is Henry Hippo!!

So as you can see, the moral of this story is to not be selfish, or only think of yourself, for in the long run, if you're honest and true, good luck will find it's way to you.

The End

In each of these pieces the *Children's Writing and Publishing* program format used was story with a heading. A graphic of the students' choice was placed to the right, and to the left in the heading the words "Buddy Writing," along with the word by and the students' names, were entered. Letter text was written by first one and then the other student alternating as they reflected on their year together.

A.

Dear Farhana, I liked working with you.

Dear Kaycee, I liked workingwith you too.

Farhana, you have talked to me better instead of being shy.

Kaycee, you were nice when you were working with me.

Farhana, you have improved your keyboarding in the period I was working with you.

Kaycee, you explained things to me that I didn't understand well.

Farhana, you have learned to read better when you had to read at the end of the writing.

Kaycee, you gave me good ideas when I was writing.

Farhana, you have drawn pictures that were really good.

Kaycee, you have gave me something to write when I was stuck and had nothing to write.

B.

Dear John,

I think your ideas have become more creatiave and interesting as the school year went by.

Dear Matt,

If I did not have you, I could not survived.

John, I enjoyed having you as a buddy very much and I think that I could have any fun having another partner.

Matt, I joyed having you as a buddy very much.

John, Your writing has improved very much and is very good now.

Love, Matt and John

C.

Dear Theodore I like working with you.

Dear Tallulah I like working with you too because you gave good comments to me.

I also liked working with you, Theodore, because I felt responsible teaching someone.

You were friendly to me most of the times, Tallulah.

The times I worked with Theodore he worked nicely and listened to me.

Tallulah was creative.

Theodore was cooperative.

PROMPT 21. FOUR INTENTS OF WRITING

Note: These samples present the scripts written to accompany a single set of field trip slides taken during a tour of Annapolis, MD. The scripts, based on the four intents of writing, illustrate how writing for different purposes impacts the finished piece. A different group of students writing cooperatively produced each of the scripts.

Our Trip to Annapolis

A. Narration
1. One day while the fourth grade was touring Annapolis, commotion broke out on the floor of the House. The representatives had gone to get Colonial artifacts and found them missing.
2. People were doing research to determine exactly what was missing. They were checking the video tapes on security cameras and computer data bases.
3. Delegate Counihan explained to us there was a problem and he asked us to come with him.
4. He gave us the facts about what happened. It seems that some historical artifacts have been discovered missing. Delegate Counihan asked us to find the criminal and missing artifacts and bring them back to the State House.
5. Inside the desk he told us we would find a walkie-talkie book. We took it with us so we could contact him in time of need or when we had information to share.
6. Since we needed information, we went to the Information Desk. The data disc was missing. We heard footsteps and a door slam.

7. We followed the sounds up the stairs and lost sight of the criminal. We decided to check the Old Senate room for clues.

8. We noticed the pocket of George Washington's coat was inside out. There was an ink smudge on it. We determined the money, ink, the pipe and his hat were all missing. We decided to go outside for some fresh air and to think.

9. We overheard a man telling two women he was going to be rich soon. They asked why and he said, "I came across something very ancient and valuable. Now I am going to get what I deserve."

10. We decided to follow our suspect because he was very suspicious. He went around the old Treasury Building and we followed.

11. He cut through the backyard of a house with seven gables.

12. We saw him on the sidewalk. When he turned the corner we lost sight of him.

13. Looking at the map we pinpointed where we thought the man was going next.

14. We asked the tour guide where the address we saw on the map was. She told us how to find it.

15. We knocked on the door of the house and waited to see who answered. The man who came out was the man we had overheard talking to the women.

16. We asked him to show us the artifacts in his bag. He told us about the clay tavern pipe and how it was used. We thought we were on to something so we activated the walkie-talkie book.

17. Next he described the Colonial money.

18. He showed us his ink packet and told us about how you used a tussy mussy. We accused him of stealing the artifacts from the Old Senate Chamber.

19. The suspect grabbed his bag and started running toward the Liberty Tree.

20. He continued running past the statue of Tecumseh.

21. The chase continued through Bancroft Hall.

22. He cut through the St. John's campus disrupting the croquet game.

23. Then the man ran into the flower shop and handed the bag to the owner saying, "I got what you wanted, now give me my money!" We used our walkie-talkie book and called the police for help. They came and arrested both the crooks.

24. We took the artifacts and headed back to the State House.

25. We hoped we might get a reward when we returned the artifacts.

B. Persuasion

1. Learn more about how our Maryland government is run. Witness for yourself how our laws are made.

2. Admire this beautiful legislative room. See how technology is used in our government.

3. If you are a Marylander, observe your delegates and senators in action. If you are real lucky, visit with one of them.

4. Experience how it feels to sit in one of your delegate's desks as you tour the State House. Observe the beautiful portraits of former speakers of the House of Delegates.

5. If you're fortunate, your guide might allow you to sit in the desk of your delegate. You will enjoy seeing the buttons your delegate uses in voting.

6. A trip through the underground tunnel will be a real surprise for you. At the end of the tunnel you'll find the information desk. Browse through the many Maryland pamphlets and brochures.

7. Enjoy seeing the marble staircase that was imported from France. Its beauty will amaze you.

8. Observe the place Washington stood as he resigned his Commission. It will make you think you were there. Look for the women's balcony, the Georgian architecture, and authentic, antique furniture. Your tour guide will tell you all about this historical happening.

9. Take a scenic tour of old Annapolis. The cost is minimal. You'll see many neat objects. The guides will tell you a lot of interesting facts.

10. You'll find out information about how early Colonists used security safeguards.

11. Savor the beauty of an old Annapolis home full of history.

12. Stroll down the brick streets of Annapolis. Browse in the antique shops and old Colonial buildings. Relive the feelings of the 1700s.

13. Learn to move about the city easily with this helpful map. Discover important places to visit.

14. The tour guides will give you important information about wars early Marylanders fought. They will tell you how the people lived.

15. Experience the elegant Georgian architecture in some of our old houses. You will notice it is symmetrical on both sides.

16. You will have a great time with your tour guide as you visit 18th century Annapolis.

17. You will learn about Colonial money.

18. You will learn how early Colonists added water to dry ink. Find out how people used tussy mussys.

19. The liberty tree at St. John's College will get your attention. Here you will find where William Paca and the Sons of Liberty had their secret meetings.

20. A penny thrown into the quiver gets mid-shipman a grade of C or better. Guides will tell you more about the Naval Academy.

21. Visit the largest dormitory in the U.S. it is here at the Naval Academy.

22. If you come on the special Saturday in the fall you will hear the cheers of the crowd as you witness the cadets playing St. John's College in a game of croquet.

23. Visit this interesting flower shop.

24. Be amazed as you view the beautiful dome of the Maryland State House.

25. Visit and appreciate our state capital. We hope you have a wonderful time at our city, Annapolis.

C. Informative

1. The Maryland legislature is where our laws are made. There are two chambers. One is the State Senate and the other is the House of Delegates. In the House of Delegates chamber, in this picture, delegates are sharing ideas.

2. Some people work after the meeting is adjourned.

3. Delegate Gene Counihan is the delegate who represents Montgomery County District 15 in the General Assembly. He often shows school children around the State House.

4. Delegate Counihan took fourth graders from Damascus Elementary School onto the floor of the House of Delegates. They learned how a bill becomes a law. He also showed everyone the desks and let the students see what it is like to sit in the delegates' seats.

5. Delegate Counihan showed the students the buttons on the desks and explained what the buttons were used for. They were used for voting and for calling a page. The red button is used for "nay." The green button stands for "yes." The white button stands for "erase."

6. People can get information on bills at this desk.

7. This staircase leads from the first floor to the second floor of the State House. it is very wide and is made of marble. A famous painting of George Washington resigning from the Continental Army is at the top of the stairs.

8. In the old part of the State House some special things happened. In the Old Senate Chamber George Washington resigned as Commander-in-Chief of the Army. In the same place Thomas Jefferson was appointed to be our first ambassador. The Treaty of Paris was also approved here. That treaty ended the Revolutionary War. Some of the furniture in this room is the original furniture from the 1700s.

9. Three guides in costume took fourth graders around Annapolis. These are the clothes that Colonial people wore in the 1700s.

10. The first Treasury Building in Annapolis still stands next to the State House.

11. This is an old house in Annapolis. It has seven gables.

12. There are many old houses and brick streets in Annapolis. The sidewalks and streets are narrow.

13. Annapolis was designed with two circles. They are called State Circle and Church Circle. Streets cross the circles and if you look at them on a map they look like spokes on wheels.

14. Women in Colonial times wore long dresses and bonnets on their heads. A bag was tied around their waist. It was used as a pocket.

15. Many of the old houses were symmetrical. This was called Georgian architecture.

16. In the Colonial days many people smoked the same pipe. They just broke off the end when a different person wanted to smoke it.

17. Tobacco backed up the money in Colonial Maryland. In Maryland we had six dollar and eight dollar bills. We would accept money from other Colonies.

18. A tussy mussy is a little bag filled with spices. Since everyone took baths only twice a year, they smelled bad. When someone met a friend on the street, they held the tussy mussy up to their nose while they said hello. That way they didn't smell the other person.

19. The Liberty Tree is where the Sons of Liberty would meet to plot against the King of England. It is on the grounds of St. John's College. The Sons of Liberty would meet there so no one would hear their discussions. Every Colony had a Liberty Tree. Our tree is one of the last Liberty Trees that survive.

20. A statue of the Indian Tecumseh is on the Naval Academy grounds. The midshipmen believe that if they throw a penny into the quiver, they will get a good grade on their exam. Every holiday they paint the statue different colors.

21. Bancroft Hall is where the midshipmen live at the Naval Academy. it is the biggest dormitory in the United States. Each room is kept very neat and clean. Two midshipmen live in every room. Each person has a bed, a closet, a desk, and a chair. There is a shower attached to the room. The rooms are not air conditioned.

22. St. John's College is near the State House. This college doesn't have regular classes and tests. The students read many books. They meet with tutors to talk about their books. The Liberty Tree and the Liberty Bell are on the grounds of St. John's College. Croquet is their favorite and only sport. They play against the Naval Academy.

23. A small flower shop is located across the street from St. John's College.

24. The State House has a wooden dome that is the largest wooden dome in the United States. It is put together with wooden pegs because they did not have metal nails in Colonial times. The wood that was used is cypress wood because termites do not like it. This dome has two layers of wood with stairs inbetween so that someone can raise and lower the flags each day. There are two flags on the top, the United States flag and the Maryland flag. The dome also has an acorn on the

top that stands for wisdom so the senators and the delegates will make wise choices.

25. Our State House is the oldest State House in the United States that is in continuous use for making laws. The state house in Boston is older, but it is no longer used for making laws. The old part of our State House was built in the 1700s and the new section was built in the 1900s. The State House is an example of Georgian architecture, where both sides are symmetrical. In addition to the General Assembly, the Governor has his office there.

D. Feelings

1. We felt important because not many fourth graders get to go in there. It smelled old and musty. It had a very high ceiling.

2. The lady on the computer looked bored.

3. Nobody knows how to act around Delegate Counihan since he is special.

4. We felt comfortable because the seats were very soft. When we looked in the desks we saw things like candy, cigars, and papers.

5. On the desks there were buttons and switches. We were tempted to push the buttons, but we were afraid security might get mad at us.

6. We were wondering what kind of information they had and why anyone would choose such a boring job.

7. The stair case looked very expensive. It would be neat to slide down the bannister. Kids were afraid they would fall over the bannister.

8. In the Old Senate Chamber, the waxed figure of George Washington looked spooky because he looked real!

9. The guides in costume looked funny because their fashion was way out of this century.

10. The Treasury Building was so tiny that we wondered how they could fit all the tobacco into it. It looked odd to see two chimneys on such a small building.

11. The gables were as green as cucumbers.

12. The streets and buildings looked so old that we felt sorry for the people who lived and worked there.

13. The map was hard to understand but fortunately there was an arrow that said "You are here." Unfortunately, it did not help because it was pointing to the floor.

14. The lady in costume looked weird because she dressed from Colonial times. She told a sad story of a time when she and her husband were so hungry that they had to kill her pet rabbit for food d.

15. A Georgian Architect made a stupid mistake by putting two door-knobs differently on the door. They were supposed to be symmetrical.

16. The guide with the pipe had a very expressive face. He moved his eyebrows up and down when he spoke.

17. We were tempted to steal the old money from the guide, but he looked too innocent.

18. We laughed at the thought of people not bathing for a year. We thought the tussy mussy didn't work because it didn't smell. It needed new spices.

19. We wondered how the Liberty Tree was still living after 400 years. The guide told a story of how the students of St. John's College had blown a hole in the tree as a prank. It really did the tree a favor because it blew all the bugs and diseases out of the tree.

20. We hoped that if we threw a quarter at the statue of Tecumseh we would get an A on our next test. It looked like Tecumseh had snakes on his head.

21. The room in Bancroft Hall looked the opposite of all our rooms. It was so spotless that it made us sick. We couldn't imagine living like that.

22. St. John's College looked boring because they only had only two sports.

23. The flower shop was called the Flower Box. It was as small as a box and looked like a box of flowers.

24. Looking up at the steeple in the State House made us all feel like fleas. It was so high up that it looked like it was going to fall on us especially when the clouds were moving.

25. We felt proud to be Marylanders as we looked at our State House.

Samples of Revision Process

Note: Given below are an initial draft (A), additional information requested through the peer conferencing process (B), and revision based on that conference (C). These examples are the work of a single student.

A.

My Room
In my room is a bed. Nest to it is a table. I have a rug my grandmother made for me. There is a closet along one wall. Off of my room is a bathroom. My great grandmother's trunk is between the windows.

B.

Bed. The bed was my grandfather's. The bed is walnut. My grandfather was over six feet tall so he had the bed lengthened. It is called a spool bed because of the way the wood spindles are shaped.

Table. The table is walnut. I keep a phone on it. My clock radio is there, too. I keep a book on it to read when I go to bed. There is a lamp on the table.

Picture. The picture was painted in China. It is called 100 Butterflies. There are butterflies and flowers on it. It is painted on silk.

Trunk. The trunk was my great grandmother's. It is made of wood and leather. I keep my yarn and needlepoint projects in it. It has a fancy key in its lock.

Room. There are two windows. All along one wall is a built-in closet. There is a bathroom connected to my room. The sun comes in the windows in the morning.

Rug. On top of the carpet is a rug my grandmother made. It is made out of clips cut from old woolen clothes. The clips are knotted on string and sewn together. It has a lot of colors mixed in it.

C.

My Room

When you walk into my room you see my bed. It is an antique bed which was my grandfather's. It is made of wood. I have a table next to my bed with a lamp and a telephone on it. My clock radio is on the table, too. Across the room is a storage trunk. It was my great grandmother's. She used it to bring her belongings to the United States from England. I keep yarn and other craft projects in it. All along one wall is a closet. It has doors that slide to open and close. On top of the carpet is a special rug. My grandmother made it. She cut old clothes into little strips and knotted them together. There are interesting patterns and colors in the rug. The best part is that I can find pieces of my favorite clothes from when I was younger.

Note: Sample drafts shown below illustrate the difference between revising and editing. There are an initial draft (A), a first revised draft (B), and a second revised draft (C). The final step (D), editing, corrects spelling, punctuation, paragraphs, capitalization, etc. These examples are the work of a single student moving through the processes.

A. FIRST DRAFT: GET IDEAS DOWN

Pants vs. Dresses for School

I like wearing pants better for lots of reasons. Dresses are OK, but it what goes with wearing them is not. Pants have pockets so you dan carry important items with you like yout keys and money. Some dress have pockets, but things are more likely to fall out. YOu can sit without thinbking in pants. Skirts flop around and can be embarasing. The worst thing about wearing dresses is all the things you have to wear under them and on your feet. Slips and pantry hose are the wotrst. ALso dressy shoes are not as comfortable and your legs get cold. Pants can be for play like jeans or better like slaks and pant suites. It is easy to get dressed waring pants. Just pull on a shirt and pull on the pants. You are ready to go.

B. FIRST REVISION: FOCUS ON CONTENT, CLARITY, AND ORGANIZATION

I like wearing pants to school better than wearing dresses for lots of reasons. Dresses are OK, but it is what goes with wearing them that is not. The woorst thing about wearing dresses is all the things you have to wear under them and on your feet. Slips and pantry hose are the wotrst. Also dressy shoes are not as comfortable on your feet. In the winter your legs get cold wearing dresses. Most dresses do not have pockets. If they do have pockets they are small and let things fall out easily. YOu have to be careful how you sit when wearing a dress. The skirt can flop around and be embarasing. Panats on the other hand have manay advantages. It is easy to get dressed wearing pants. Just pull on a shirt and pull on the pants and you are ready to go. Pants cover your lgs so you don't get cold in the winter. Pants have pockets so you can cary important items with you like yout keys and money. You cana't lay them down and lose them like you can a purse. You don't have to think about the way you are sitting when you are wearing pants. You can sit on the floor or with your legs crossed without worring. Pants can be for play like jeans or better iike slaks and pant suites. Recess is a lot more fun when you wear pants. You don't have to remember what day is PE if you are in the habit of wearing pants you are all set.

C. SECOND REVISION: FOCUS ON SENTENCE STRUCTURE AND VOCABULARY

Wearing pants to school rather than dresses has a number of advantages. Wearing a dress is OK, but it is what goes along with wearing one that creates the drawbacks. The biggest drawback is all the garments you have to wear with a dress. Slips and panty hose are the worst. Your feet are not as comfortable in dressy shoes and your legs get cold waiting for the bus in the winter. Another drawback to dresses is their lack of pockets. If they do have pockets they are usually small and let important items fall our easily. Finally you have to be careful how you sit when wearing a dress. The skirt can flop around and be embarrassing, particularly during games at recess and in PE class. On the other hand, wearing pants to school has many advantages. To begin with it is easier to get dressed in the morning. Just pull on a top and pull on the pants and you are ready to go. Everything goes with jeans and cords you don't havea to consider what matches what. Wearing panats your legs don't get so cold at the bus stop in the winter. The best advantage is secure pockets for important items such as keys and money. Pants pockets are usually deep enough to keep treasures from falling out. You can organize your belongings by using several pockets rather than having everything fall to the bottom of a purse. Relying on pockets avoids a major disadvantage of a purse, laying it down and loosing it. That never happens to pockets. Wearing pants you can sit on the floor or cross your legs without worrying. Recess is a lot more fun when you wear pants because you can skin the cat and climb on the monkey bars. You don't have to remember what daya PE falls on if you are in the habit of wearing pants. You are always ready. Panats like jeans can be for play or for better ocasions wyou can wear slacks or pant suites.

D. FINAL DRAFT: FOCUS ON SPELLING, PUNCTUATION, AND FORMAT

Wearing pants to school, rather than dresses, has a number of advantages. Wearing a dress is OK, but it is what goes along with wearing one that creates the drawbacks. The biggest drawback is all the garments you have to wear with a dress. Slips and panty hose are the worst. Your feet are not as comfortable in dressy shoes and your legs get cold waiting for the bus in the winter. Another drawback to dresses is their lack of pockets. If they do have pockets they are usually small and let important items fall our easily. Finally, you have to be careful how you sit when wearing a dress. The skirt can flop around and be embarrasing, particularly during games at recess and in PE class.

On the other hand, wearing pants to school has many advantages. To begin with it is easier to get dressed in the morning. Just pull on a top and pull on the pants and you are ready to go. Everything goes with jeans and cords. You don't have to consider what matches what. Wearing pants, your legs don't get so cold at the bus stop in the winter. The best advantage is secure pockets for important items such as keys and money. Pants pockets are usually deep enough to keep treasures from falling out. You can organize your belongings by using several pockets rather than having everything fall to the bottom of a purse. Relying on pockets avoids a major disadvantage of a purse—laying it down and loosing it. That never happens to pockets. Wearing pants you can sit on the floor or cross your legs without worrying. Recess is a lot more fun when you wear pants because you can skin the cat and climb on the monkey bars. You don't have to remember what day PE falls on if you are in the habit of wearing pants. You are always ready. Pants, like jeans, can be for play or for better occasions you can wear slacks or pant suits.

Second Example of Revision Process

A. ROUGH DRAFT: GET IDEAS DOWN

How Houdini Got Her Name

I got a cat from the shelter. They told me her name was Ellie but I knew I would change it. She hid when I brought her home. I saw her food eaten and she used her box but I never saw her for over a wekek. I wanted a lap cat and was not happy. Now Houdini thinks the only reason for me to be home is to provide her a lap to sit on. She doesn't like it when I work at the computer and turn the printer on. I pulled evrything out of the storage area under the stair because I thought she was hiding there but she wasnb't. I saw insulation pulled down from the basement ceiling at the side wall. I thought she must be hiding in the firewall. When the man I got her from came with her favorite food she came out of hiding. When he left I lost her again. I finally blocked off her ways to hide under the stairs so she went into a crawlspace by walkaing on the heat ducts. It was weeks before she began to sit on the couch with me. Houdini is a grey and white cat who doesn't like to go outside much.

B. FIRST REVISION: FOCUS ON CONTENT, CLARITY, AND ORGANIZATION

Two years ago a grey and white cat came into my house and life. I needed a cat to replace Mooch who had died of old age. The man at the shelter told me he had found this cat in his neighborhood and named her Ellie. I was sure I would change her name as I had never liked Ellie as a nickname myself. When I brought her into the house she walked around a bit and when I wasn't looking found a place to hide. She ate the food I put down for her and used her box, but I never saw her or heard a sound for a week. I looked for her all over the house. Twice I pulled almost everything out of a storage area under the basement stairs. I pokek around what was seft and etermined she was not hiding there. I looked up and noticed some insulation hanging down next to a hole in the firewall up next to the ceiling. I thought that must be her hiding place. I didn't see how she could get in and out. I called the man from the shelter and explained my problem. he agreed to come to the house and try to catch her with a "have-a-heart" trap baaited with her favorite food. When the cat heard his voice she came out of hiding. She had been under the stairs but escaped my searches. It took many attempts before I succeeded in sealing off her escape routes back into hiding. At that point I realized I was refering to her as being like Houdini the great escape artist. When she found her way blocked she chose a new hiding place. She walked across the basement floor, hopped up on the washing machine, hopped to the top of the water heater and from there walked along the heating ducts to an crawl space above a closet. She spent the next few weeks looking down at me from there. By now I was calling her Houdini. I had wanted a lap cat. This was not working out well at all. She would have nothing to do with me. I was just about ready to take her back when she hopped up on the couch with me. Little by little she stopped hiding and began spending more and more time with me. Now Houdini seems to think the only reason for me to be home is to provide her with a lap.

C. SECOND REVISION: FOCUS ON SENTENCE STRUCTURE AND VOCABULARY

Two years ago a grey and white cat came into my house and has rearranged my life. I needed a cat to replace Mooch who had recently died of complications related to old age. The man at the shelter told me he had found this cat in his neighborhood and named her Ellie. I was sure I would change her name as I had never liked Ellie as a nickname myself. I have found cats earn their names so I decided to wait and watch her for a while. I was sure the right name would become obvious. When I brought her into the house she walked around a bit and when I wasn't looking found a place to hide. She regularly ate the food I put down for her and used her box, but I never saw her or heard a sound from her for a solid week. I kept searching for her all over the house. Twice I pulled almost everything out of a storage area under the basement stairs. I pokek around what was left and determined she was not hiding there. I looked up and noticed some insulation hanging down from the ceiling next to a hole in the cinder block firewall. I thought that must be her hiding place, but I didn't see how she could get in and out. I called the man at the shelter and explained what had happened and my theory about where she was hiding. He agreed to come to the house and try to catch her with a "have-a-heart" trap baited with her favorite food. When the cat heard his voice she came out of hiding. She had been under the stairs but escaped my searches. It took many attempts before I succeeded in sealing off her escape routes back into hiding. At that point I realized I was referring to her as being like Houdini the great escape artist. When she found her way blocked it wasn't long before she chose a new hiding place. She walked across the basement floor, hopped up on the washing maching, next to the top of the water heater and from there she walked along the heating ducts to an unfinished crawl space above a closet. She spent the enxt few weeks looking down at me from there. By now I realized I was calling her Houdini. I had wanted a lap cat. This was not working out well at all. She would have nothing to do with me. I was just about ready to take her back when one Sunday evening she hopped up on the couch with me while I watched TV. Little by little she stopped hiding and began spending more and more time with me. Now Houdini seems to think the only reason for me to be home is to provide her with a lap. She earned her name with her initial behavior, but cpontinues to deserve it as she enjoys getting into small places and ambushing me from secret hiding places.

D. FINAL REVISION: FOCUS ON SPELLING, PUNCTUATION, AND FORMAT

Two years ago a gray and white cat came into my house and has rearranged my life. I needed a cat to replace Mooch who had recently died of complications related to old age. The man at the shelter told me he had found this cat in his neighborhood and named her Ellie. I was sure I would change her name as I, myself, had never liked Ellie as a nickname. I have found cats earn their names so I decided to wait and watch her for a while. I was sure the right name would become obvious.

When I brought her into the house she walked around a bit and when I wasn't looking found a place to hide. She regularly ate the food I put down for her and used her box, but I never saw her or heard a sound from her for a solid week. I kept searching for her all over the house. Twice I pulled almost everything out of a storage area under the basement stairs. I poked around what was left and determined she was not hiding there.

I looked up and noticed some insulation hanging down from the ceiling next to a hole in the cinder block firewall. I thought that must be her hiding place, but I didn't see how she could get in and out. I called the man at the shelter and explained what had happened and my theory about where she was hiding. He agreed to come to the house and try to catch her with a "Have-a-Heart" trap baited with her favorite food.

When the cat heard his voice she came out of hiding. She had been under the stairs but escaped my searches. It took many attempts before I succeeded in sealing off her escape routes back into hiding. At that point I realized I was refering to her as being like Houdini the great escape artist.

When she found her way blocked it wasn't long before she chose a new hiding place. She walked across the basement floor, hopped up on the washing maching, then to the top of the water heater, and from there she walked along the heating ducts to an unfinished crawl space above a closet. She spent the next few weeks looking down at me from there. By now I realized I was calling her Houdini.

I had wanted a lap cat. This was not working out well at all. She would have nothing to do with me. I was just about ready to take her back to the shelter when one Sunday evening she hopped up on the couch with me while I watched TV. Little by little she stopped hiding and began spending more and more time with me. Now Houdini seems to think the only reason for me to be home is to provide her with a lap. She earned her name with her initial behavior, but continues to deserve it as she enjoys getting into small places and ambushing me from secret hiding places.

REFERENCES

Introduction

1. Hannum, Wallace. "Reconsidering Computer Literacy: Is It a Basic Skill?," *Education Digest* (January 1992): 11.
2. Davidson, Jan. As quoted by Keith Ferrell in "Conversations," *Compute* (January 1991): 24.
3. Bixby, Lenore. Conversation with author, Collington, Mitchellville, MD, February, 18, 1991.
4. Appell, Michael W. "Computers in Schools: Solution or Disaster?," *Education Digest* (February 1992): 48.
5. _____. 49.
6. _____. 52.
7. Brent, Rebecca and Richard M. Felder. "Writing Assignments—Pathways to Connections, Clarity, and Creativity." *College Teacher* (Spring 1992): 43.

Chapter 1: Integrating the Use of Computer Programs with Other Learning Materials

1. Snyder, Tom. *Critical Thinking in the Classroom*, guide to simulations program *Decisions, Decisions* series, Cambridge, Massachusetts, 1988: 2.

2. Skapura, Robert. "A Primer on Automating the Card Catalog," *School Library Media Quarterly* (Winter 1990): 75.

Chapter 2: Linking Thinking Skills with Writing

1. Machias, William Clark. *Electronic Learning* (May/June 1992): 8.

2. Walter, Kate. *Chance to Succeed*: *An Afternoon Tutorial Program*. New York: Plan for Social Excellence, Inc., 1991, 21.

3. Hines, Cronin. "Combining Writing with Text Organization in Content Instruction." *AASCP Bulletin* (March 1992): 35.

4. _____. 44.

5. Dorazio, Patricia. "Writing Lab's Network Encourages Peer Review and Refinement," *THE Journal* (April 1992): 73–74.

6. Cowan, Hilary. *Electronic Learning* (May/June 1992) 21.

7. Hill, Maggie. "Writing to Learn Process Writing Moves into the Curriculum," *Electronic Learning* (Nov./Dec. 1992)

8. Hollingsworth, Helen. *Electronic Learning* (Nov./Dec. 1992): 18.

9. Fogarty, Robin. "Ten Ways to Integrate the Curriculum," *Educational Leadership* (Oct. 1991): 56.

10. Pilchman, Beverly. "Technology Links to Literacy," *Reading Teacher* (April 1992): 654.

11. Winograd, Ken. "What Fifth Graders Learn When They Write Their Own Math Problems.." *Educational Leadership* (April 1992): 65–66.

12. _____. 65.

13. Miller, Diane. "Begin Mathematics Class with Writing," *Mathematics Teacher* (May 1992): 354.

14. Gmuca, Jacqueline L. "Reading, Writing, and Thinking: The Work of Eloise Greenfield and the Development of Critical Thinking Skills."

Paper presented at the Annual Meeting of the National Council of Teachers of English (77th, Los Angeles, CA, November 200–25, 1987): 7.

15. Jackson, Roberta. "The Untapped Power of Student Note Writing," *Educational Leadership* (April 1992): 54.

16. Brent, Rebecca and Richard Felder. "Writing Assignments—Pathways to Connections, Clarity, and Creativity;." *College Teacher* (Spring 1992): 43

17. _____. 43.

18. _____. 45

Chapter 3: Facilitating Teacher Use

1. Shields, Mark H. *Using Computers to Improve Writing Skills and Attitudes of Middle School Students* (1991) M.S. Practicum, Nova University: 23.

2. Fidanque, Ann. "Keyboarding Tips." *The Computing Teacher* (May 1990): 37.

3. Anderson-Inman, Lynne. "Computers and the Language Arts." *The Computing Teacher* (May 1990): 34.

Chapter 5: Families' Participation

1. Polin, Linda. "Current Thinking About Critical Thinking: Implications for Technology Use." *The Computing Teacher* (February 1991): 7.

Chapter 8: Evaluating Student Output

1. Bunce-Crim, Marna. "Evaluation: New Tools for New Tasks." *Instructor* (March 1992): 23.

2. _____. 24.

3. Baker, Eva L. and Robert L. Linn. "Writing Portfolios: Potential for Large Scale Assessment." Project 2.4: *Design Theory and Psychometrics for Complex Performance. Assessment. Design and Analysis of Portfolio*

and Performance Measures. Los Angeles, CA: National Center for Research on Evaluation, Standards, and Student Testing, 1992. Preface.

4. Bunce-Crim, Marna. "Evaluation": 28.

5. _____. 26

6. Baker, Eva L. and Robert L. Linn. "Writing Portfolios": 12n.

7. Bunce-Crim, Marna. "Evaluation": 24

8. Baker, Eva L. and Robert L. Linn. "Writing Portfolios": 7–8.

9. Henkin, Roxanne Lee. "Twelve Frequently Asked Questions about Writing Programs." *Illinois Reading Council Journal* (Fall 1984): 35

10. Committee on Primary Education. *Responding to Children Writing.* Edinburgh: Scottish Curriculum Development Service, 1986: 44.

11. Henkin, Roxanne Lee. "Twelve": 35.

12. Committee on Primary Education. *Responding to Children*: 47.

13. Arkansas State Dept. of Education, Little Rock. "McRAT Report" (January 1991): 2.

14. Hoctor, Marge. *Teaching with Technology.* Canoga Park, CA: California Associataion for the Gifted, 1991: 2.

15. Arkansas State Dept. of Education, Little Rock. "McRAT Report" (January 1991): 3.

16. White, Edward M. *Assessing Higher Order Thinking and Communication Skills in College Graduates through Writing.* Commissioned paper prepared for workshop of same name (Washington, DC, November 17–19, 1991) in support of National Education Goal V, Objective 5.

17. Simpson, Mary K. "What Am I Supposed to Do While They're Writing?" *Language Arts* (November 1986): 680.

18. _____. 681–684.

19. Brown, H. J., Jr. *P.S. I Love You.* Nashville, TN: Rutledge Hill Press, 1991: 23.

20. Harp, Bill. "When The Principal Asks "When You Do Whole Language Instruction, How Will You Keep Track of Reading and Writing Skills?" *The Reading Teacher* (November 1988): 160.

21. _____. 161.

22. Bunce-Crim, Marna. "Evaluation:" 25.

23. *Writing to Read 1988–89.* Brooklyn, NY: New York City Board of Education, Office of Research, Evaluation, and Assessment, 1990 : 24.

24. Bryson, Mary and Marlene Scaradamalia. "Teaching Writing to Students at Risk for Academic Failure" in *Teaching Advanced Skills to Educationally Disadvantaged Students.* Urban Education. NY: Columbia University Teachers College, 1991: 54.

25.   White, Edward M. *Assessing Higher Order Thinking*: 2.

26.   Committee on Primary Education. *Responding to Children:* 16.

27.   _____. 23.

28.   _____. 23.

29.   _____. 26.

30.   _____. 26.

31.   White, Edward M. *Assessing Higher Order Thinking*: 11.

32.   _____. 6.

INDEX

Simulation, 3
Site licenses, 24
Space, 20
Spell checker, 4
Spelling, 84
Staffing, 15
Statistics, 34
Story poems, 51
Story problems, 9, 52, 54
Strengths of computer, 10
Student datadiscs, 23
Support, 14, 15, 32
Supporting details, 70

T

Team effort, 13
Technology, 78
Thanksgiving activity, 58
Three times rule, 11
Time zones, 53
Timelines, 1
Touch typing, 16

U

Uniform procedures, 23
Utility programs, 1

V

Verb vocabulary, 58
Verbs, 41
Vocabulary development, 2, 38, 39, 57, 69, 76
Volunteers, 16, 27

W

Water cycle, 77
Web, 8
Whole language, 84
Wiring, 20
Word processing, 4, 9
Word rich climate, 84
Writing instruction, 7
Writing proficiency, 83